# Laughing Boy

## by Stephen Unwin

Based on the book *Justice for Laughing Boy*
## by Sara Ryan

Performed at Jermyn Street Theatre, London,
from 25 April - 31 May 2024

# Laughing Boy
## by Stephen Unwin

Based on the book *Justice for Laughing Boy* by Sara Ryan

**Cast**

| | |
|---|---|
| SARA RYAN | Janie Dee |
| OWEN | Lee Braithwaite |
| CONNOR | Alfie Friedman |
| WILL | Charlie Ives |
| RICH | Forbes Masson |
| ROSIE | Molly Osborne |
| TOM | Daniel Rainford |

**Production Team**

| | |
|---|---|
| Writer and Director | Stephen Unwin |
| Author | Sara Ryan |
| Designer | Simon Higlett |
| Lighting Designer | Ben Ormerod |
| Sound Designer | Holly Khan |
| Video Designer | Matt Powell |
| Casting Director | Ginny Schiller CDG |
| Associate Director | Ashen Gupta |
| Assistant Director | Sam Chown-Ahern |
| Associate Sound Designer | Anna Wood |
| Assistant Video Designer | Douglas Baker |
| Fight Director | Enric Ortuño |
| | |
| Production Manager | Lucy Mewis-McKerrow |
| Stage Manager | Daisy Francis-Bryden |
| Technical Assistant Stage Manager | Grace Hancock |
| Costume Supervisor | Rachael Griffin |
| Production Carpenter | Basement 94 |
| Production Technician | Ted Walliker |
| | |
| Executive Producer | David Doyle |
| Producers | Gabriele Uboldi |
| | Kate Johnson |

## Thanks

Special thanks to Sara Ryan and her family: Rich, Rosie, Will, Owen, Connor and Tom; everyone in the #JusticeforLB campaign; George Julian; the families of Andrew Marber, Chris Nota, Coco Bradford, Colette McCulloch, Danny Tozer, Danny Willgoss, Edward Hartley, Jared Botham, Jessie Eastland-Seares, Joe Ulleri, Kristy Saleh, Laura Booth, Matthew Copestick, Peter Seaby, Richard Handley, Sally Lewis, Sammy Alban-Stanley, Sasha Forster, and Thomas Rawnsley; Elise Robinson, Luis Martinez Betancor and the Queensmill at Fulham Cross Academy Choir; the Joey team; Access All Areas; Go Live Theatre Projects; Turtle Key Arts; Unicorn Theatre; Zoo Co Theatre; Caroline Wilkes; David Harling; Kelly Hunter; Lauren Thorpe; Ramandeep Kaur; and Toby Sams-Friedman.

Audio introduction supported by Unity Theatre Trust.

Rehearsal space supported by Jerwood Space.

# Cast

### Janie Dee | Sara Ryan

Theatre includes: *Stephen Sondheim's Old Friends* (Gielgud Theatre); *The Motive and the Cue*, *Follies* (National Theatre); *The Grass is Greener* (Theatre Royal Windsor); *An Hour and a Half Late* (Theatre Royal Bath); *Vanya and Sonia and Masha and Spike* (Theatre Royal Bath/Charing Cross Theatre); *A Little Night Music* (Buxton Opera House); *The Boyfriend* (Menier Chocolate Factory); *Pinter 4: Moonlight/Night School* (The Jamie Lloyd Company/Harold Pinter Theatre); *Monogamy* (Park Theatre); *Hand to God*, *The Seagull* (Regent's Park Theatre); *Dream Queen* (Sam Wanamaker Playhouse/London Festival of Cabaret); *Ah, Wilderness!* (Young Vic); *84 Charing Cross Road* (Salisbury Playhouse); *A Little Night Music* (Palace Theatre); *A Midsummer Night's Dream* (Russia/China/Shakespeare's Globe).

Television includes: *The Burning Girls* (Paramount+); *You & Me* (ITV); *Song for Nature* (Sky Arts); *Chimerica* (Channel 4); *Crashing* (Channel 4/E4); *Doctor Who*, *A Tribute to Harold Pinter*, *The Murder Room* (BBC); *Celebration* (CBC).

Film includes: *Official Secrets* (Classified Films); *The Trouble With Dot and Harry* (Existential Films); *Dare to be Wild* (Oasis Films); *Me and Orson Welles* (CingmaNX).

Janie Dee is winner of multiple Olivier, Evening Standard, Critics' Circle, Obie, Theatre World Newcomer and TMA Theatre Awards.

### Lee Braithwaite | Owen

Theatre includes: *Cowbois* (RSC/Royal Court Theatre).

Film includes: *We Live in Time.*

### Alfie Friedman | Connor

Theatre includes: *The Witches of Eastwick* (The Sondheim Theatre).

Television includes: *The Undeclared War* (Channel 4/Peacock).

### Charlie Ives | Will

Theatre includes: *Babies and Bathwater* (A Pinch of VAULT); *A Christmas Carol – A Ghost Story* (Nottingham Playhouse/Alexandra Palace); *Private Lives* (Ambassadors Theatre, West End); *Miss Popplewell's Garden* (The Rude Mechanicals); *Mrs Warren's Profession* (Theatre Royal Bath); *The Show Must Go On* (Vienna's English Theatre); *We Never Get Off at Sloane Square* (Drayton Arms Theatre); *Sherlock Holmes: An Online Adventure* (Les Enfants Terribles); *Tabby McTat* (ABA International UK/Hong Kong/Singapore); *The Internet Was Made for Adults* (VAULT Festival).

Television includes: *The Puppet Master: Hunting the Ultimate Conman* (Netflix).

**Forbes Masson | Rich**

Previously for Jermyn Street Theatre: *Farm Hall* (Bath Theatre Royal/UK Tour).

Theatre includes: *Jekyll and Hyde* (Royal Lyceum Edinburgh/UK Tour); *Newsies!* (Troubadour Theatre); *The Taxidermist's Daughter* (Chichester Festival Theatre); *The Magician's Elephant*, *The Boy in the Dress*, *Macbeth*, *Hamlet*, *The Comedy of Errors*, *Twelfth Night*, *The Histories*, *As You Like It*, *Romeo and Juliet*, *The Taming of the Shrew*, *The Grain Store*, *Morte d'Arthur*, *The Pilate Workshop Project*, *Ahasverus*, *Tender Thing* (RSC); *Summer and Smoke* (Almeida Theatre/Duke of York's Theatre); *Little Shop of Horrors* (Regent's Park Theatre); *Travesties* (Menier Chocolate Factory/Apollo Theatre); *Mr Foote's Other Leg* (Hampstead Theatre/Theatre Royal Haymarket); *Doctor Faustus* (Duke of York's Theatre); *Macbeth*, *Richard II*, *The Ruling Class* (Trafalgar Studios/Jamie Lloyd Productions); *Big Fish* (The Other Palace); *King Lear* (Liverpool Everyman/Young Vic/Headlong); *The Lion, the Witch and the Wardrobe* (Kensington Gardens); *Bartholomew Fair*, *The Merry Wives of Windsor*, *Boudica* (Shakespeare's Globe); *Dumbstruck*, *Terror* (Lyric Hammersmith); *Art*, *The Breathing House*, *Stiff* (Lyceum Edinburgh); *As You Like It*, *Romeo and Juliet* (RSC Residency in New York); *Life of Stuff* (Donmar Warehouse); *Laurel and Hardy* (Edinburgh Festival/Wellington Festival NZ); *The Trick is to Keep Breathing*, *The Real World*, *Cinzano* (Tron Theatre Glasgow).

Television includes: *The Crown* (Netflix); *Royal Mob* (History); *As You Like It* (CBeebies/Globe); *Irvine Welsh's Crime* (BritBox); *EastEnders*, *Father Brown*, *Doctors*, *Shetland*, *Monarch of the Glen*, *Rab C Nesbitt*, *City Lights*, *Hamish Macbeth*, *Dead Boss*, *Supergirly*, *Red Dwarf*, *The High Life* (BBC); *Taggart* (STV); *Catastrophe*, *The Young Person's Guide to becoming a Rock Star*, *Halfway to Paradise* (Channel 4).

Radio includes: *Doctor Who: Wages of Time*, *Doctor Who: Girl, Deconstructed*, *Jago and Lightfoot* (Big Finish); *The Rise of the Nazis*, *Macbeth*, *The Tempest*, *Nuremberg*, *Catastrophic Injury*, *Behind Closed Doors*, *The Red Gauntlet*, *Waverley*, *The Fair Maid of Perth*, *The Quest of Donal Q*, *Stevenson in Love*, *Pinkerton*, *Conan Doyle – A life in Letters*, *To Throw Down God*, *Scones and Tea with V and B*, *The Forbes Masson Half Hour* (BBC); *Raj* (Audible); *The Marlowe Sessions* (L6L21).

Films include: *The Road Dance*; *Gypsy Woman.*

Writing includes: *Stiff* (Tron Glasgow/Lyceum Edinburgh); *The High Life* (BBC); *Victor and Barry* (Edinburgh Festival/Donmar Warehouse/Sydney Opera House); *Mince* (Dundee Rep); *At Home with Feste* (RSC); *Jack and The Beanstalk*, *Cinderella*, *Weans in the Wood*, *Snow White* (Tron Glasgow); *Crackers* (Belgrade Theatre, Coventry).

Forbes Masson trained at RSAMD in Glasgow (now The Royal Conservatoire of Scotland). Forbes is an associate artist with the RSC and National Theatre of Scotland. Forbes is currently writing *The High Life – The Musical* with Alan Cumming and Johnny McKnight for NTS.

**Molly Osborne | Rosie**

Theatre includes: *The Curious Case of Benjamin Button* (Southwark Playhouse); *The Sex Party*, *Indecent* (Menier Chocolate Factory); *Fiddler on the Roof* (Playhouse Theatre).

Television includes: *Call the Midwife* (BBC).

Short films include: *Path to Ecstasy*, *Eschet Chayil*.


**Daniel Rainford | Tom**

Theatre includes: *Noises Off* (Birmingham Rep/UK Tour); *Mr Burns: A Post-Electric Play* (Derby Theatre); *Surfacing* (VAULT Festival); *When Darkness Falls* (UK Tour); *Private Peaceful* (Nottingham Playhouse); *Once Upon a Time in Nazi Occupied Tunisia* (Almeida Theatre); *I Don't Dance* (So&So Arts); *AAAAA* (Lion & Unicorn Theatre); *Horseshoes for Hand Grenades* (East Riding Theatre); *Bromley Bedlam Bethlehem* (Old Red Lion); *Me And My Left Ball* (Tristan Bates Theatre).

Radio includes: *A Kestrel for a Knave* (BBC Radio 4).

Television includes: *Doctors* (BBC).

Film includes: *The Batman*, *Cost of Living*, *Catflap*.

# Creative Team

### Stephen Unwin | Writer and Director

Stephen Unwin is an award-winning British theatre and opera director. He has directed almost 100 professional productions and worked with many well-established actors and singers, as well as developing the careers of many younger ones.

In the 1980s he worked at the Almeida Theatre, the Traverse in Edinburgh, in repertoire theatre and at the National Theatre Studio. In 1993, he founded English Touring Theatre, for whom he directed more than 30 productions of classical and new plays, many of which transferred to London. In 2008, he became Artistic Director of the new Rose Theatre in Kingston, which he ran until January 2014. He has directed more than 20 operas.

Stephen has taught in conservatoires and universities in Britain and America and written 10 books on theatre and drama, including *Poor Naked Wretches*, a study of Shakespeare's working people (Reaktion, 2022). He has also written five original plays (*All Our Children* was premiered at Jermyn Street Theatre in 2017, and staged in New York in 2019) and numerous translations. He previously directed *Farm Hall* at Jermyn Street Theatre in March 2023.

Stephen is a campaigner for the rights and dignities of learning-disabled people and is completing a new book on the representation of learning disabilities in culture and society.

www.stephenunwin.uk

Twitter: @RoseUnwin

### Sara Ryan | Author

Sara Ryan is Connor Sparrowhawk's mother and a Professor of Social Care, Manchester Metropolitan University. Her scholar-activism, working with people with learning disabilities, autistic people, family carers and their allies, is gently guided and shaped by Connor and numerous other young people who should still be with us.

### Simon Higlett | Designer

Theatre includes: *Coram Boy*, *The Chalk Garden*, *The Norman Conquests*, *Nicholas Nickleby*, *Amadeus* (Chichester Festival Theatre); *Tosca*, *Falstaff* (Grange Festival); *Il Barbiere di Siviglia* (Garsington Opera); *Don Giovanni The Magic Flute*, *Le Nozze di Figaro* (Scottish Opera); *Resurrection* (Houston Grand Opera); *Saturday Night Fever* (Denmark); *The Merry Wives of Windsor* (Stockholm); *Mrs Warren's Profession* (Washington D.C); *Charlie and the Chocolate Factory*, *Chitty Chitty Bang Bang* (Leeds Playhouse/UK Tour); *Enemies*, *Whistling Psyche*, *The Earthly Paradise* (Almeida Theatre); *Accidental Death of an Anarchist* (Donmar Warehouse);

*The Force of Change* (Royal Court Theatre); *Haunted* (New York); *Pygmalion* (Old Vic Theatre); *Twelfth Night, Love's Labour's Lost, Love's Labour's Won, Singer, A Russian in the Woods, Thomas More* (RSC); *The Brothers Karamazov, Yerma* (Royal Exchange Theatre, Manchester); *Les Liaisons Dangereuses, Anna Karenina* (Gate Theatre Dublin); *Darwin in Malibu* (Hampstead Theatre); *Private Lives, Noises Off, The Price* (Theatre Royal Bath/West End); *Singin' in the Rain* (International Tour); *Derren Brown: Showman, Big The Musical; Blithe Spirit* (USA); *An Ideal Husband, The Resistible Rise of Arturo Ui, Yes, Prime Minister, Rosencrantz and Guildenstern Are Dead, When We Are Married, The Rivals, Man and Boy, Amy's View, Hay Fever* (West End).

### Ben Ormerod | Lighting Designer

Previously for Jermyn Street Theatre: *Farm Hall* (Theatre Royal Bath/UK Tour).

Theatre includes: *Manon Lescaut, The Rake's Progress* (English Touring Opera); *Carmen* (Into Opera Festival); *Wuthering Heights* (Royal & Derngate/UK Tour); *The Whale, The Double, Intimate Apparel, Trouble in Mind, Dead Kid Songs* (Ustinov Studio, Theatre Royal Bath); *Kidnapped* (National Theatre of Scotland); *The Beekeeper of Aleppo, Assassins* (Nottingham Playhouse/UK Tour); *Joyce's Women* (Abbey Theatre); *House of Desires, The Dog in the Manger* (Royal Shakespeare Theatre, Golden Spanish Age Season); *The Sex Party* (Menier Chocolate Factory); *A Christmas Carol, The Duchess of Malfi, Long Day's Journey into Night, The Oresteia, Hamlet, King Lear* (Citizens Theatre); *Don Juan* (Perth Theatre); *Prism* (Birmingham Rep/UK Tour); *Uncle Vanya, Loyalty* (Hampstead Theatre); *All's Well That Ends Well* (Sam Wanamaker Playhouse); *A Midsummer Night's Dream* (Regent's Park Open Air Theatre); *Zorro* (West End/US/Netherlands/Japan); *Mrs Henderson Presents* (Theatre Royal Bath/West End/Canada).

### Holly Khan | Sound Designer

Previously for Jermyn Street Theatre: *Jules and Jim.*

Theatre includes: *Sylvia* (English Theatre Frankfurt GMBH); *A Child of Science* (Bristol Old Vic); *Blackout Songs, This Much I Know, Biscuits for Breakfast* (Hampstead Theatre); *Tess* (Turtle Key Arts/Sadler's Wells); *Dreaming and Drowning* (Bush Theatre); *I Really Do Think This Will Change Your Life* (Mercury Theatre, Colchester); *Duck* (Arcola Theatre); *Northanger Abbey, Red Speedo* (Orange Tree Theatre); *The Invincibles* (Queen's Theatre Hornchurch); *Unseen Unheard* (Theatre Peckham); *Mansfield Park* (Watermill Theatre); *The Beach House* (Park Theatre); *For a Palestinian* (Bristol Old Vic/Camden People's Theatre); *Amal Meets Alice* (Good Chance Theatre Company/The Story Museum); *Kaleidoscope* (Filskit Theatre Company/Southbank Centre/Oxford Playhouse); *Ticker* (Alphabetti Theatre, Newcastle/ Underbelly, Edinburgh/Theatre503).

Film and Installation work includes: *Becoming An Artist: Bhajan Hunjan* (Tate Kids); *One Day* (Blind Summit Theatre/Anne Frank Trust); *Sanctuary*

(Limbic Cinema/Stockton Arts Festival); *Song for the Metro* (The Sage Music Centre, Newcastle); *It's About Time* (UN Women/Battersea Arts Centre/Mayor of London); *Their Voices* (RAA & Global Health Film Festival, Barbican).

Holly is a British/Guyanese composer, sound designer and multi-instrumentalist. Creating scores for theatre, film and installation.

### Matt Powell | Video Designer

Theatre as Video Designer includes: *RIDE* (The Old Globe, San Diego/Leicester Curve/Southwark Playhouse); *Sherlock and the Poison Wood* (Watermill Theatre); *Exhibitionists* (King Head Theatre); *I Really Do Think That This Will Change Your Life* (Mercury Theatre, Colchester); *Rebecca* (Charing Cross Theatre); *Animal* (Hope Mill Theatre/Park Theatre); *Accidental Death of an Anarchist* (Theatre Royal Haymarket/Sheffield Theatres/Lyric Hammersmith); *Blow Down* (Leeds Playhouse); *Rumi: The Musical* (D'asha Performing Arts Festival/London Coliseum); *How a City Can Save the World* (Sheffield Theatres); *A-Typical Rainbow* (Turbine Theatre); *Flight* (Royal College of Music); *But What If You Die* (Camden People's Theatre); *Old Friends* (Digital); *Bloody Difficult Women* (Riverside Studios); *Santa Must Die* (Alphabetti Theatre); *Magdalene* (Arcola Outside); *Snowflake* (The Lowry); *34* (Aria Entertainment/The Lowry); *Public Domain* (Vaudeville Theatre/Southwark Playhouse); *The Blazing World* (University of the Arts, Philadelphia); *On Hope: A Digital Song Cycle* (The Other Palace); *Plaza* (Royal Central School of Speech and Drama); *American Idiot* (Derby Theatre).

Theatre as Director includes: *Santa Must Die* (Leeds Playhouse/Red Ladder); *Nativity: The Musical, Crazy For You* (Derby Theatre); *The Unconventionals* (VAULT Festival); *Is He Musical?* (Leicester Curve/The Other Palace).

Matt is a non-binary, Offie finalist video designer, musical theatre creative and queer practitioner based in the East Midlands. They are a PhD candidate at the University of Wolverhampton researching, creating and producing LGBTQ+ representation. They trained at Royal Central School of Speech and Drama and are represented by NR1Creatives.

www.matt-powell.co.uk

### Ginny Schiller CDG | Casting Director

Ginny has been an in-house casting director for the RSC, Chichester Festival Theatre, Rose Theatre Kingston, ETT and Soho Theatre and has worked closely with Bath Theatre Royal and Ustinov Studio for the last decade. She has cast extensively for the West End and touring circuit as well as for the Almeida, Arcola, Birmingham Rep, Bolton Octagon, Bristol Old Vic, Cambridge Arts, Charing Cross Theatre, Clwyd Theatr Cymru, Frantic Assembly, Hampstead Theatre, Headlong, Jermyn Street Theatre, Leicester Curve, Liverpool Everyman and Playhouse, Lyric Theatre Belfast, Menier Chocolate Factory, Northampton Royal & Derngate, Nottingham

Playhouse, Oxford Playhouse, Plymouth Theatre Royal and Drum, Regent's Park Open Air Theatre, Shakespeare's Globe, Shared Experience, Sheffield Crucible, Traverse Edinburgh, West Yorkshire Playhouse, Wilton's Music Hall, Young Vic and Yvonne Arnaud Guildford. She has also worked on many television, film and radio productions, including the BBC Radio 4 series *Nuremberg* and *Nazis: The Road to Power*. Some recent productions include *Noises Off* with Felicity Kendal and Matthew Kelly, *A View from the Bridge* directed by Lindsay Posner with Dominic West, *The Curious Case of Benjamin Button* at Southwark Playhouse, *Machinal* directed by Richard Jones at the Ustinov Studio, Theatre Royal Bath, and Old Vic, *The Starry Messenger* at the Wyndham's, *The Best Exotic Marigold Hotel* directed by Lucy Bailey, *Bad Jews* at the Arts Theatre and *Farm Hall* and *All Our Children* directed by Stephen Unwin at Jermyn Street.

### Ashen Gupta | Associate Director

Theatre and opera includes: *Brown Sheep* (VAULT Festival); *Carmen*, *Gloriana* (London Coliseum); *Chasing Hares*, *Khab Jeetigi* (Young Vic); *Jack and the Beanstalk* (Stratford East); *NW Trilogy* (Kiln Theatre); *Pygmalion* (Evolution Festival, Lyric Hammersmith); *The Promise* (UK Tour).

Film for theatre includes: *I Threw It* (Old Vic); *Jineologî* (Shoreditch Town Hall); *Living Newspaper* (Royal Court); *TWENTYTWENTY* (Young Vic).

### Sam Chown-Ahern | Assistant Director

Theatre includes: *Astronauts*, *Other: Please Specify* (Platform Islington).

Television includes: *Are You Autistic?* (Channel 4).

Film includes: *The Stimming Pool* (2023).

Sam trained at Wimbledon College of Arts (UAL).

### Anna Wood | Associate Sound Designer

Theatre includes: *To Be Continued* (Little Fish Theatre); *Dance Nation* (ALRA); *A Streetcar Named Desire* (Almeida Theatre/West End); *Party Time/Celebration*, *Bang Bang Bang* (Royal Central School of Speech and Drama); *A Christmas Getaway* (Lichfield Garrick Studio); *Romeo and Juliet* (Cambridge Arts Theatre).

Anna trained as a composer at the Royal Welsh College of Music and Drama.

### Douglas Baker | Assistant Video Designer

Previously for Jermyn Street Theatre: *Boy in Da Korma*.

Theatre includes: *The Promise* (Deafinitely Theatre); *Mandrake* (R&D); *Hot in Here* (Gate Theatre); *The Butterfly Project* (Undone Theatre); *Agrippina* (Jackson's Lane); *The Sleeping Sword* (Watermill Theatre); *The Prince*

(Southwark Playhouse) *Ten Days in a Madhouse*, *A Christmas Carol*, *Moby Dick* (Jack Studio Theatre); *Faust* (Lazarus Theatre R&D); *Castles Palaces Castles* (Prague Quadrennial).

Film includes: *The End of It*, *Mise en Abyme*.

Douglas is a disabled, interdisciplinary theatremaker. Since 2017, at So it Goes Theatre, he has created and directed accessible work utilising video design in unusual local venues. In February 2023, he won the Offie Video Design Award and a Standing Ovation 'Most Innovative New Play' Award for *Ten Days in a Madhouse*. In April 2023, a selection of his work was exhibited as part of Hello Stranger Yorkshire at Leeds Playhouse. Douglas uses video to transform audience perspective, creating an illusion of action and interaction between video and performer, and to activate spaces scenographically. Douglas is a Creative Associate at Jermyn Street Theatre.

### Daisy Francis-Bryden | Stage Manager

Previously for Jermyn Street Theatre: *Farm Hall*, *Footfalls and Rockaby* (Theatre Royal Bath); *Orlando*.

Theatre includes: *The Barber of Seville* (Wilton's Music Hall); *Sleeping Beauty Takes a Prick* (Charing Cross Theatre); *Salty Irina* (Roundabout @ Summerhall); *Play AI* (Riverside Studios); *Who's Holiday* (HOME/Southwark Playhouse); *UK Drill Project* (Barbican Pit Theatre); *Horse-Play* (Riverside Studios); *The Man in the Moon* (St Paul's Church/Belcombe Court); *Originals: Live at Riverside Studios* (Riverside Studios); *The Night Woman* (The Other Palace); *On The Line* (London Schools Tour); *GirlPlay* (Camden People's Theatre); *The Duration* (Omnibus Theatre).

Daisy is a freelance Stage Manager. Since graduating in 2021, they have worked on a variety of productions, predominately as Company Stage Manager and Deputy Stage Manager.

### Grace Hancock | Technical Assistant Stage Manager

Theatre as Assistant Stage Manager includes: *Jack and the Beanstalk* (Royal Spa Centre, Leamington Spa); with Book Cover, *TONY! The Tony Blair Rock Opera* (Leicester Square Theatre/UK Tour); as ASM Deputy, *Disney's The Lion King* (UK Tour); in training, *London Road* (Dame Shirley Bassey Studio); *The Writer* (Sherman Studio, Sherman Theatre); *Twelfth Night Remembered* (Bute Theatre); *Così fan tutte* (Dora Stoutzker Hall).

Theatre as Deputy Stage Manager in training includes: *The Dog in the Manger* (Bute Theatre).

Theatre as Stage Manager in training includes: *Freedom [March on Selma]* (Bute Theatre/The Yard Theatre); *Abigail's Party* (Caird Studio); *La Dama Boba* (Bute Theatre).

Theatre as Technical Swing in training includes: *Anna Karenina* (Bute Theatre).

Having graduated from Royal Welsh College of Music and Drama's Stage Management and Technical Theatre course in 2022, Grace enjoys working across a variety of different projects, with experience across musicals, touring, and family theatre.

### Rachael Griffin | Costume Supervisor

Theatre includes: *Jungle Book* (Chichester Festival Theatre).

Rachael is a freelance set designer, researcher and costume assistant.

### Theatre Royal Bath Productions

Theatre Royal Bath consists of an historic Main House, the Ustinov Studio and the Egg Theatre.

Theatre Royal Bath Productions is the Theatre Royal Bath's commercial production arm, and one of the most prolific British theatre producers in the West End, on UK tour and internationally. We have produced over 250 plays and productions since our inception, including more than 40 West End transfers.

West End credits include: *The Birthday Party* (Piccadilly Theatre); *Entertaining Mr Sloane, Romeo and Juliet, Happy Days, Oleanna* (Arts Theatre); *The Beau, The Rivals, The Libertine, A View from the Bridge* (Theatre Royal Haymarket); *Up for Grabs*; *Quartermaine's Terms, Relatively Speaking, The Price* (Wyndham's Theatre); *Abigail's Party* (New Ambassadors/Whitehall Theatre/Wyndham's Theatre); *Betrayal, Fences* (Duchess Theatre); *The Dresser, The Judas Kiss, Hay Fever* (Duke of York's Theatre); *You Never Can Tell, Amy's View* (Garrick Theatre); *The Importance of Being Earnest, The Deep Blue Sea, Private Lives, Hobson's Choice, Stepping Out, The Mentor* (Vaudeville Theatre); *Legal Fictions* (Savoy Theatre); *Pygmalion, Machinal* (Old Vic); *Enjoy* (Gielgud Theatre); *The Caretaker, Another Country* (Trafalgar Studios); *Mrs Warren's Profession* (Comedy Theatre); *Blithe Spirit, The Madness of George III* (Apollo Theatre); *Relative Values, Blithe Spirit, Four Quartets* (Harold Pinter Theatre); *Speed-the-Plow* (Playhouse Theatre); *Bad Jews* (Arts Theatre/Theatre Royal Haymarket); *The Father* (Wyndham's Theatre/Duke of York's Theatre); *Mrs Henderson Presents* (Noël Coward Theatre); *Switzerland, Private Lives* (Ambassadors Theatre); *Noises Off* (Phoenix Theatre/Theatre Royal Haymarket).

# The West End's Studio Theatre at 30

Jermyn Street Theatre is a unique seventy seat theatre in Piccadilly Circus. World-class, household-name playwrights, directors and theatrical legends like Siân Phillips and Trevor Nunn work here alongside those taking their first steps in professional theatre. It is a crucible for multigenerational talent.

We stage world premieres, rare revivals, and reimagined classics and collaborate with theatres across the world. Our productions have transferred across the UK, to Broadway and beyond.

30 years ago in 1994, Howard Jameson and Penny Horner (who continue to serve as Chair of the Board and Executive Director today) created the theatre out of what had been the staff changing room for the restaurant upstairs with no core funding. Since then, the theatre has flourished thanks to a mixture of earned income from box office sales and the generosity of individual patrons and trusts and foundations. In 2017, the theatre became a full-time producing house. We won the Stage Award for Fringe Theatre of the Year in both 2012 and 2021.

Caroline Quentin in *Infamous*.
Photography by Steve Gregson.

Archie Backhouse, Forbes Masson and Daniel Boyd in *Farm Hall*. Photography by Alex Brenner.

# JERMYN STREET THEATRE 30

# Support Us *at* 30

Wondering what to get us for our big birthday? Your Friendship makes the best present of all!

Over the last 30 years, we've made a name for ourselves as the West End's Studio theatre. With just 70 seats, **our small scale is our greatest strength**: a unique place where artists can afford to take risks and audiences can afford to see the work.

But even with every seat filled, **ticket sales only generate 60%** of what we need to build our productions, fund our small team, and champion the next generation of artists. We rely on the generosity of donors like you for the remaining 40%. **Your support ensures we can build on the legacy of the last three decades** and make the next 30 years the most exciting yet.

## Lifeboat Friends

(From £4.50 a month)

Our **Lifeboat Friends** are the heart of Jermyn Street Theatre. Benefits include:
- Dedicated Priority Booking period.
- Invitation to a Friends Night for each production, with a chance to meet the cast.

## The Miranda Club

(From £45 a month)

Members of **The Miranda Club** enjoy all the benefits of the Ariel club, plus:
- Acknowledgment in our Front of House.
- Annual Friends Lunch with our Artistic Director.
- Invitation to one Press Night/Gala Night per year.
- Behind-the-scenes access and a closer relationship with our team.

## The Ariel Club

(From £12.50 a month)

**Ariel Club** members receive all the benefits of Lifeboat Friends, plus:
- Chances to attend Press Nights.
- Complimentary signed programme or playtext for each production.
- Acknowledgement in programmes, playtexts, and on our website.

## The Director's Circle

(From £250 a month)

The **Director's Circle** is an inner circle of our most generous donors. They are invited to every Press Night and enjoy regular informal contact with our Artistic Director and team. The first to hear our plans they often act as a valuable sounding board.

To join us, visit, www.jermynstreettheatre.co.uk/friends/
Jermyn Street Theatre is a Registered Charity No. 1186940

# Our Friends

## The Ariel Club

Richard Alexander
Derek Baum
Martin Bishop
Dmitry Bosky
Katie Bradford
Nigel Britten
Christopher Brown
Donald Campbell
James Carroll
Ted Craig
Jeanette Culver
John Dale
Shomit Dutta
Jill & Paul Dymock
Bernard Fleckney
Lucy Fleming
Anthony Gabriel
Carol Gallagher
Roger Gaynham
Paul Guinery
Debbie Guthrie
Diana Halfnight
Julie Harries
Eleanor Harvey
Andrew Hughes
Jennifer Jacobs
Margaret Karliner
David Lanch
Caroline Latham
Isabelle Laurent
Christine MacCallum
Keith Macdonald
Vivien Macmillan-Smith
Nicky Oliver
Kate & John Peck
Lydia Petty
Adrian Platt

Alexander Powell
Oliver Prenn
Mart Ralph
Martin Sanderson
Carolyn Shapiro
Nigel Silby
Philip Somervail
Gary Trimby
George Warren
Lavinia Webb
Ann White

## The Miranda Club

Anonymous
Anthony Ashplant
Gyles & Michèle Brandreth
Marcia Brocklebank
Sylvia de Bertodano
Robyn Durie
Richard Edgecliffe-Johnson
Nora Franglen
Mary Godwin
Louise Greenberg
Ros & Alan Haigh
Phyllis Huvos
Mark Jones
Pauline Kelly
Marta Kinally
Yvonne Koenig
Hilary King
Jane Mennie
Dr Tiziana Morosetti
Charles Paine
John & Terry Pearson
Iain Reid
Ros Shelley
Martin Shenfield

Carol Shephard-Blandy
Jenny Sheridan
Sir Bernard Silverman
Brian Smith
Frank Southern
Mark Tantam
Paul Taylor
Geraldine Terry
Brian & Esme Tyers

## Director's Circle

Anonymous
Philip Carne MBE &
Christine Carne
Jocelyn Abbey &
Tom Carney
Colin Clark RIP
Lynette & Robert Craig
Gary Fethke
Flora Fraser
Robert & Pirjo Gardiner
Charles Glanville &
James Hogan
Crawford & Mary Harris
Ros & Duncan McMillan
Leslie & Peter MacLeod-
Miller
James L. Simon
Peter Soros & Electra Toub
Fiona Stone
Melanie Vere Nicoll
Robert Westlake &
Marit Mohn DBE

# LAUGHING BOY

Stephen Unwin

Adapted from Sara Ryan's *Justice for Laughing Boy*

*To All the Young Dudes*

### A Beautiful Boy, a Book and an Ink Pad
*Sara Ryan*

Connor died. He should be alive.

### The Book

The book I wrote about what happened – *Justice for Laughing Boy* – was launched at Doughty Street Chambers six years ago with a wonderful panel of Helena Kennedy, Caoilfhionn Gallagher KC and Deb Coles, Director of the charity INQUEST. I wore a red scarfy-thing knitted by the mum of one of Connor's teaching assistants. Members from the Oxfordshire-based self-advocacy group My Life My Choice including their President, Michael Edwards, sat in the front row and cheerfully chipped in.

Writing the book was an exercise in love and witnessing. I'd written a blog for years. Writing joy, laughter, critique and commentary. The book was a way of capturing Connor as a person and trying to make sense of the responses to his death. Following the blog, it went from hilarity and joy to utter devasation, documenting the brutality of the investigatory processes and bullshit (or worse) families face when someone dies in state 'care'. It was written before some of these processes ended (they never end).

### An Ink Pad

I was uncomfortable at the thought of being asked to sign copies of the book (what do you write?) and made a stamp with a tiny bus image to avoid this. The ink pad still works. I didn't stamp or sign many copies in the end. Rich, Rosie, Will, Owen, Tom and George Julian had complimentary copies. I sent a copy to Michael's sister down Dorset way. He persuaded the publisher to produce a audiobook version at the launch.

**The Play**

Steve Unwin began to talk about a play before lockdown. He loved the book and started work to bring it to the stage. We met in Oxford. There was further discussion, draft scripts, potential news, updates and undates. I approached this in the same way I dealt with the book. As a kind of interested bystander with a stamp and an ink pad. Vaguely surprised when the play was mentioned, passing on updates to family and friends with caveats; this may not happen.

A few months ago Steve shared the most recent version of the script (a corker) and news the play, *Laughing Boy*, would be on at Jermyn Street Theatre followed by a week at Bath. Wow. A meeting was held with Stella Powell-Jones and David Doyle (Artistic Director and Executive Producer) in a London pub to talk about the important stuff.

How to get this right. That was the discussion. With Thai curry.

The announcement was made on a Thursday lunchtime. *The Lonely Londoners* in Feb/March followed by *Laughing Boy* in April/May. I was at a writing retreat at Gladstone's Library distracted by the beauty of the mushrooms as details bounced around social media.

So many messages and posts. A buzz of action, excitement and anticipation despite everything else going on. 'Would it go up North?' 'Highlight of next year!' 'My Life My Choice are bussing to Bath.' 'Brilliant,' said Norman Lamb. My mate Becca got her clipboard back out to organise the life-raft trip to London. Booked. Booked. Booked.

Someone prosaically tweeted, 'Lots of time to do something remarkable.'

It's already remarkable. A beautiful boy dismissed in life matters. His quirkiness, love of life and buses, humour, irreverence and courage to stick two fingers up at adversity count.

I'm setting aside my stamp and ink pad. There will be tears. So many tears, alongside laughter, bafflement and kick-ass brilliance.

Thank you, Steve Unwin.

**Precious Cargo:**
**Adapting *Justice for Laughing Boy* for the Stage**
*Stephen Unwin*

I can't remember when I first heard about Connor Sparrowhawk and his dreadful death. I remember meeting his mother, Sara Ryan, at a disability event sometime in 2015 and watching the #JusticeforLB campaign develop on social media and in the press and did the little I could to support it. But, to my shame, it wasn't until I read her brilliant book *Justice for Laughing Boy* in 2018 that I really started to understand what had happened and why it mattered so much.

In some ways the story felt personal. My second son Joey is just a year younger than Connor, and, like Connor, has learning disabilities and epilepsy. Like Connor he needs help with certain things. And like Connor he generates enormous joy in his family and friends, and laughter and love surround him wherever he goes.

But there the similarities end. Because what happened to the eighteen-year-old Connor is that he was taken from his family home and plunged into a hell that is almost impossible to comprehend.

Slade House in Oxford (now thankfully closed) was what is known as an Assessment and Treatment Unit, one of the deeply dysfunctional NHS institutions set up to help (mostly) autistic people whose care has broken down and who could benefit from a short and focused intervention.

The awful fact is, however, that these places are not fit for purpose, and people are often locked away in them for months, years even, largely forgotten about, except by their desperate families who do whatever they can to get them out.

Connor spent one hundred and seven miserable and lonely days in Slade House: no proper assessment was made, no treatment was offered, his freedoms were restricted, visits were controlled and finally, despite repeated warnings, he was left unattended in a bath where he drowned while having an epileptic seizure.

This was ten years ago: 4 July 2013.

In the face of the family's unimaginable grief, a growing campaign for justice was created, not just to establish Southern Health's (frequently denied) responsibility for this entirely avoidable death of a healthy young man, but to expose the many cases of neglect, cruelty and abuse which is still so often the experience of people in a wide range of medical, educational and residential institutions.

This homegrown campaign was a model of its kind, drawing together people of good will from many different backgrounds and skills, who found themselves confronted by an appalling culture of corporate buck-passing, dead-eyed denial and the vilest kind of victim blaming.

But eventually, the world took notice.

And so, a few years ago, I set out to dramatise the story for the stage: not just to tell audiences about what happened to Connor and his family, but to help them understand the challenges faced by so many people with learning disabilities and their families today.

It was a strange feeling trying to give dramatic shape to a group of people who are – with one tragic exception – very much still with us. I was determined to respect their experiences and allow audiences to feel something of their grief, their rage, and their determination to create a better world. But, of course, I knew it also had to be a vivid drama. Striking the right balance was hard.

Fortunately I had two things on my side.

The first was Sara Ryan's book which tells us so much about the everyday life of Connor and his family. She lets us in in a way which is honest, revealing and, as with all the best writing, rich with contradiction. She offers an overwhelmingly powerful and detailed account of what led up to her son's death and even intersperses the book with brief imaginary dialogues with

Connor which I have been able to transfer almost verbatim. She also explains (and celebrates) how the #JusticeforLB campaign emerged and achieved so much in the face of bureaucratic obfuscation and the massed ranks of well-paid chief executives and their expensive lawyers.

I was also grateful to have Sara's unwavering support for the project and have been constantly touched by her willingness to check my factual errors, correct my misunderstandings, and prompt me to be better, bolder, and braver. I would readily understand if she felt she couldn't face revisiting the pain, but I think she knows that one of the best ways of working for the rights and dignities of people with learning disabilities today is to show just how badly things can go wrong.

Inevitably I feel a real responsibility to honour Connor's memory in the best way I can: his family, his friends and everyone who was involved in the campaign deserve no less.

*Justice for Laughing Boy* is no dusty memoir: it is a living, breathing campaign which has achieved so much. But there is still so much to do if people like my Joey are to be granted the fundamental human rights and dignities that Connor was so brutally denied.

For the dreadful fact is that the approximately one and a half million people across the country who have some level of learning disability are still forgotten, neglected and mistreated. The culture of appalling negligence and evasion described in *Justice for Laughing Boy* is everywhere to be seen, and Connor Sparrowhawk wasn't the first young person to die in an institution supposedly set up to help, and tragically won't be the last.

In 2017 I wrote a play called *All Our Children* about the Nazi persecution of disabled children which was also staged at Jermyn Street. *Laughing Boy* is its dreadful but logical sequel.

A change has to come. Maybe this play can, in some small way, help to bring that about.

**Characters**

SARA
CONNOR
RICH
ROSIE
TOM
WILL
OWEN

*And so many others*

**Notes**

Lots of doubling except for Sara and Connor. Connor must be played by an autistic and/or learning-disabled actor.

The stage as a stage. Clean floor and simple chairs.

The cast on stage throughout. No costume changes or props. Lots of projections and film. Music and sound throughout. Movement.

A lively collage which captures the bewilderment, the confusion, the shifts and complexities of the story. The action is very fluid and should be played straight through without an interval, and at speed. It's a terrible story but must be performed with optimism, laughter, satire and energy.

The LB quilt should be displayed in the foyer if possible.

*This text went to press before the end of rehearsals and so may differ slightly from the play as performed.*

**PART ONE: BEFORE**

**1.1**

CONNOR. I died this morning.
    In the bath.
    I'm dead now.
    Am I dead, Mum?
    Mum?
    Am I dead?


**1.2**

SARA. July fourth, 2013. A Thursday. It was incredibly hot.
    And I took the bus into Oxford. As usual. Connor's bus. As
    usual.

*Text-message alert.*

Oh hang on. It's Fran.

*Reads.*

Is Connor going to the prom tomorrow?

*Typing on her phone.*

I'll ask him when I see him.

*Sends.*

But there's something I still can't remember. I know I bought
some food on the way, but was it breakfast or lunch? I put it
in the staff fridge. Which isn't the kind of thing I usually do.
But I did that day. And I've no idea why.

*Phone rings.*

Sara Ryan.

DR JAYAWANT. Oh, hello, Mrs Ryan, it's, erm, Dr Jayawant from the Unit.

SARA. Oh hello.

DR JAYAWANT. Is this a good time to talk?

SARA. I think so. I've just, erm –

DR JAYAWANT. Lovely day, isn't it?

SARA. It's so hot.

DR JAYAWANT. Look, it's about Connor. He's been, erm, taken into the JR.

SARA. The what?

DR JAYAWANT. The hospital, that's right, and erm –

SARA. Yes?

DR JAYAWANT. Well, he was found unconscious in the bath.

SARA. Is he okay?

DR JAYAWANT. Oh, there's nothing to worry about. The airway was cleared before he left. His key worker is with him and he'll ring if there are any developments.

SARA. And I remember the sun in my eyes in that open-plan office. Actually, the glass was smeared, but –

*Pause.*

And I still don't know how I got out of there. I told my colleague Caroline what had happened and I walked faster and faster towards the hospital. Where's that bloody bus stop?

CAROLINE. But I decided to call a cab and go with her.

SARA. And the cab crawled along the Banbury Road. And it was so bloody hot. And I couldn't remember if she said he was conscious or not. And, Caroline, what if he's in a coma? What will that do to his – ?

CAROLINE. Look, we don't know what's happened. Try to take it one step at a time –

SARA. We're here.

SARA *arrives at the hospital.*

CONSULTANT. Oh hello, Mrs Ryan. Look, I'm terribly sorry, but your son is on a ventilator in the resus room.

And I'm afraid –

SARA. Yes?

CONSULTANT. – There's nothing we can do.

SARA. What did you say?

CONSULTANT. I'm so sorry.

SARA. In the – ?

CONSULTANT. Yes, just through here.

SARA. Through there?

I think the consultant understood. But at that moment, standing in A&E, I understood nothing. Life was in slow motion. Everything was spinning round.

I can't –

I just can't –

*Blurry footage of kids with a range of neuro and physical disabilities singing and signing Louis Armstrong's 'What a Wonderful World' by Bob Thiele and George David Weiss. Fragments of this punctuate the action from time to time.*

Look at that lot. When things are right, when people are kind, they have no limits. Such beautiful, beautiful kids. Oh, what a wonderful world it could be. What a –

Oh fuck.

*Sobbing.*

**1.3**

REPORTER. So, Ms Ryan, how would you describe your son?

SARA. Connor?

REPORTER. Yes, what was he like?

SARA. I don't know. Erm –

REPORTER. Surely you can –

SARA. He's Connor. He –

REPORTER. But what was he like?

*Pause.*

SARA. Rich, what would you say?

RICH. Quirky? I don't know. He was great.

SARA. Tom?

TOM. Could be bloody annoying. But he was my big brother, so –

ROSIE. Listen, Connor was the best. The absolute best.

SARA. Rosie is Connor's big sister. She always defended him.

ROSIE. I loved him, that's all. I loved him.

REPORTER. And did he enjoy life?

CONNOR. Yeah! And I had a brilliant sense of humour. Wanker.

WILL. Oh, Connor, mate!

SARA. This is Will, Connor's brother.

WILL. We all loved you, Connor, even if you –

CONNOR. Wankers!

WILL (*playful tussling with* CONNOR). Oi!

OWEN. We used to make stuff together. Took hours.

SARA. That's Owen.

OWEN. Also Connor's brother.

TOM. Short little films with Lego and stuff. Look.

*YouTube projection.*

Cool, eh?

SARA. So, you see, Connor was, well, unusual, weren't you, matey?

CONNOR. Fuck yeah!

SARA. Choosy too.

CONNOR. Yeah!

SARA. You knew what you liked.

CONNOR. Yeah!

SARA. And what you didn't like. Why don't you tell the man what you liked?

CONNOR. I liked Chunky Stan.

RICH. That was our dog. He loved Chunky Stan.

ROSIE. And laying on the ground like a lizard, sun worshipping.

TOM. And endless clips of lorries, getting on and off cross-Channel ferries.

*YouTube projection.*

On. Off. On. Off. He loved lorries.

OWEN. He could be a bit of a handful at times.

WILL. But loads of fun. We laughed a lot.

CONNOR. Hey Tom, what are we gonna drink tonight?

TOM. I dunno, Connor.

CONNOR. The fountain of youth!

WILL. He loved to make us laugh.

SARA. Which is why we called him Laughing Boy.

WILL, OWEN, ROSIE, TOM (*laughing*). Laughing Boy!

CONNOR (*laughing*).Wankers! Wankers! Wankers!

SARA. LB for short.

RICH. He had a particular affection for septic tanks. I know, but he did. Septic tanks.

SARA. And London buses. You wouldn't believe how much Connor loved London buses. Which is why –

*The JusticeforLB image comes up.*

WILL, OWEN, ROSIE, TOM (*defiant, laughing, proud*). Justice for Laughing Boy!

CONNOR. Yeah! Justice!

SARA. Hi, I'm Sara Ryan. I'm an academic. I worked at Oxford University at the time, which is something else I never expected. Disability Studies too, ironically. Family and work have always been linked for me. Particularly as Connor broke every rule going. A 'free radical', I called him.

RICH. Here's an example. Every Saturday for about fifteen years when the kids went to the Co-op round the corner to buy sweets, Connor always wanted exactly the same thing: fruit pastilles. Always fruit pastilles.

CONNOR. I liked fruit pastilles!

RICH. And at Christmas he only ever wanted one present and ignored the rest. Completely single minded.

ROSIE. He had this police tabard which Mum got from the Early Learning Centre, and he wore it for, oh, about ten years, with bright-orange binoculars and a baseball cap. That was his gear.

CONNOR. Yeah, cool!

WILL. And he wouldn't take it off.

SARA. So, you see, Connor was, well, Connorish. That's what he was.

ROSIE. Is.

SARA. Was.

ROSIE. Is.

SARA. Drop dead gorgeous too. A bleeding rock star.

RICH. Not everybody got him, though. When Connor was two, Sara took him to a paediatrician.

PAEDIATRICIAN. Now, look, Mum –

SARA. Sara.

PAEDIATRICIAN. Yes, right, now look, Sara, there's not much that can be done, I'm afraid. Social services will be able to offer you respite as he gets older. But that's about it.

SARA. Respite?

PAEDIATRICIAN. You'll get used to it. People do.

SARA. From Connor?

PAEDIATRICIAN. And do beware of denial. It's very common, you know, especially with –

SARA. Thank you.

ROSIE. Connor didn't talk till he was about four. Mum went to the head of my primary school to see if she would give him a place there.

SARA. Her office smelt of stale hyacinths.

HEADMISTRESS. I don't think so, do you? We have very high academic standards, Sara, as you know from Rosie, and erm –

SARA. So, instead, he went to a special school about five miles from where we lived. A really lovely school. He was happy there, and he was safe. And he stayed there for the rest of his life.

Nearly.

REPORTER. So, Ms Ryan, could you tell us what Connor *didn't* like?

SARA. Well, he didn't like shops.

CONNOR. I hate shops, don't I, Mum? Do I hate shops?

SARA. You do. And too much noise.

CONNOR *blocks his ears.*

WILL. And reversing the car, you didn't like reversing the car, did you?

CONNOR. Bloody hated it.

WILL. I used to wind you up about it, didn't I?

CONNOR. Wanker!

RICH. One summer I took the kids camping. We forgot to tell Connor that he was going to be away for a couple of nights. The next morning –

CONNOR. I want to go home now. Camping's over.

RICH. So, I drove him all the way home.

SARA. And you didn't sleep much, did you, matey? Ever.

CONNOR. I hate sleeping, Mum.

SARA. So, you see, Connor had a different way of thinking.

WILL. He'd play football and was totally unfazed when he was in goal.

CONNOR. I let in a thousand goals, Mum.

WILL. He'd stand in the goal and when the ball got close, he'd just walk away.

SARA. He was, as you may have guessed, autistic. Among other things. I remember one evening I was lying in a hot bath reading something ever so clever – or it might have been *Hello!* I can't remember – and I could hear him in his bedroom playing.

CONNOR. Mum? Are you my mum, Mum?

SARA. Yes.

CONNOR. Really, Mum?

SARA. I think so. And later, interviewing autistic adults and parents of autistic kids, I realised what he was asking.

CONNOR. Mum? Are you my 'mum', Mum?

SARA. Yes, matey. I'm your mum, and I'll always love you.

REPORTER. What were his favourite things?

WILL. Tell him about Connortown.

CONNOR. Cool!

*Early Learning Centre town map.*

Buses. Lorries. Cars. Connortown. See?

REPORTER. Lovely.

CONNOR. And ConnorCo, my company.

REPORTER. Your – ?

CONNOR. Heavy haulage. ConnorCo. Like Eddie Stobart, see?

REPORTER. Tell me about the buses?

CONNOR. Loads of buses outside my window, see? Number 2, 2a, 280, 800. Oxford Tube to London City, National Express to Stansted. See?

REPORTER. And so many lorries, all lined up –

CONNOR. And coaches. D'you like buses and coaches?

REPORTER. I do.

CONNOR. Cool!

SARA. He often saw things in his own way. Hey LB! How did meal prep go today?

CONNOR. Not so good, Mum.

SARA. Oh, why?

CONNOR. I failed, Mum.

SARA. What do you mean, you failed?

CONNOR. I failed, Mum.

SARA. What did you cook?

CONNOR. Kebabs, Mum.

SARA. And what went wrong?

CONNOR. I didn't have a skewer, Mum.

SARA. Why not?

CONNOR. Dunno, Mum.

SARA. So, what did you eat for lunch?

CONNOR. Bits, Mum.

SARA. Or this: Connor, you know I love lorries? And buses and coaches –

CONNOR. Do you love lorries, Mum?

SARA. Yes.

CONNOR. Mum, do you love lorries?

SARA. Yes. And I look out for them all the time. Wherever I am.

CONNOR. Why, Mum?

SARA. Because you did.

CONNOR. I love lorries, Mum.

SARA. I know, Connor.

CONNOR. How do you know, Mum?

SARA. Because you told me.

CONNOR. Did I tell you, Mum?

SARA. Yep. All the time. All the bleeding time.


## 1.4

RICH. Holidays could be tough. One year we went down the White Scar Cave in Yorkshire. It's two miles deep and pitch black. A couple of light bulbs hanging in the gloom.

GUIDE (*reverb*). I'm just going to turn these off so you can see the stalactites.

*Suddenly dark. Handheld torch.*

CONNOR. Get me out of here. GET ME OUT NOW.

SARA. Shh… LB. Shhh. Don't be silly.

TOM. Shhhhhh…

CONNOR. Johnny English, save me. Johnny English, NOW!

ROSIE, TOM *and* SARA. Shhhhhhhhhhhhhhhhh.

CONNOR. THE ROOF'S GOING TO FALL IN. WE'RE ALL
GOING TO DIE!

SARA. Come on, let's go.

*Running into the light.*

Phew.

GUIDE. Funny little lad. Is he alright?

SARA. What did you say?

GUIDE. Well, you know.

SARA. Yes, he's alright. Hope so. Goodbye.

GUIDE. Cheerio.

SARA. But the truth is Connor was terrified and at times like
these his distress could be overwhelming. But we found
a way through, didn't we, matey?

CONNOR. Always, Mum. Always.


## 1.5

ROSIE. Let me tell you about epilepsy. Epilepsy is –

WILL. Shit.

ROSIE. Complete shit. Connor was fifteen, I think, and we were
all watching *Up* for about the hundred and fiftieth time, and
he suddenly got so worried about the granddad in the film he
lost consciousness for a moment.

RICH. You alright, Connor?

ROSIE. Connor?

OWEN. What's up, mate?

WILL. What is it?

RICH. Dunno. He's okay, now. You okay?

CONNOR. Yeah.

DEPUTY HEADTEACHER. Sara, it's the school, Connor's absolutely fine, but he's with the paramedics. We think he's had a seizure.

SARA. What?

DEPUTY HEADTEACHER. A tonic-clonic epileptic seizure. He's okay but he's been taken to the hospital to be checked over.

SARA. I ran there and beat him to it, and there he was emerging from the ambulance grinning and laughing. But it was absolutely terrifying. WILL. Epilepsy's really common in people with learning disabilities.

ROSIE. They used to say it was God's punishment.

OWEN. Or a bloody angel struggling to get out.

ROSIE. Never just epilepsy.

SARA. Connor hated his epilepsy.

CONNOR. I don't have epilepsy, Mum, I don't.

SARA. Time for your meds, matey.

*Gives him his phenytoin.*

He had epilepsy. That's for sure.


### 1.6

RICH. By the way, I'm Rich, Sara's partner. Anyway, it was my fortieth birthday and they gave me a dog. I didn't want a dog, certainly not a –

CONNOR *appears with Chunky Stan.*

– Jack Russell puppy!

CONNOR (*in a high-pitched voice*). Come on, Stan, the bus is coming, where's that bus, hey Stan, I met a really nice girl the other day, she's dead fit and she fancies me, come on, Stan –

SARA (*laughing*). Connor, don't let him lick your face –

RICH. Connor had this amazing ability to always choose the best-looking dish from the menu. What was that one you ordered at the Aziz last time, Connor, that lamb dish?

CONNOR. Lamborghini.

RICH. Brilliant.

SARA. And there was the time he came back from the Christmas market. He'd seen an American girl with a baseball cap.

CONNOR. Mum.

SARA. Yes?

CONNOR. Mum, she fancied me, Mum.

SARA. Cool.

CONNOR. She really fancied me, Mum.

SARA. Super cool. How do you know?

CONNOR. She looked at me, Mum.

SARA. Did you talk to her?

CONNOR. No, Mum, too shy, Mum. Can we go back next year, Mum?

SARA. Yeah, we'll go next year.

CONNOR. Thank you, Mum. 'To fancy or not to fancy, that is the question.'

SARA. I'd give anything to hear those jokes again.


**1.7**

RICH. It's tough for kids like Connor. Lousy services start to seem almost normal. And parents –

SARA. – especially mothers, for some reason –

RICH. – have to do stuff way above the usual. Endless paperwork, endless meetings, endlessly making the case.

SARA. And all the time the powers that be wave a dirty great stick over your head saying –

VOICE 1. A lack of resources.

VOICE 2. It's just too expensive.

VOICE 3. There are too many people who need help.

VOICE 4. There isn't a magic money tree.

SARA. Well, fuck that. I'm sorry, but our kids are worth more than that. They really are.

RICH. Luckily, we met some good people on the way. Small charities who have a real commitment. Pockets of brilliance.

SMALL CHARITY WORKER 1. Hey Connor, what do you fancy doing today?

SMALL CHARITY WORKER 2. That's such a cool T–shirt!

SMALL CHARITY WORKER 3. Let's check out that new bus.

SARA. But loads of shite too. Well-meaning but poorly thought through shite. It all starts when our kids are called 'special'.

VOICE 5. Oh, he's so special.

VOICE 6. Really special.

VOICE 7. You're all so special.

VOICE 6. Special parents get special kids.

SARA. They're not special. We're not special. Nobody's special.

RICH. Our kids are our kids. We do what we can.

SARA. Everyone's special.

*Pause.*

There was this young dentist called Dan. A really nice lad.

DAN. Hi, Connor, mate, can you just say – ?

CONNOR. Ah –

DAN. Brilliant. Really cool! All done!

CONNOR. Mum, what do you think Dan's doing right now, does he have a girlfriend, is he playing around with her, what do you think, Mum?

SARA. I don't know, Connor, and I don't know why he liked Dan so much. Nice work, Dan.

DAN. Glad I could help.

SARA. It's people like that who make all the difference. People who –

SARA, RICH, TOM, OWEN, ROSIE, WILL (*singing*).
Happy birthday to you
Happy birthday to you
Happy birthday, dear Connor
Happy birthday to you

CONNOR *blows candles out*. RICH *helps*.

SARA. I can't remember how the tradition started, but we always used to go up to London on Connor's birthday.

CONNOR. Just you and me, Mum.

SARA. Just you and me nowadays.

CONNOR. Look, Mum: a bus, a London bus, it's a Routemaster.

SARA. They must have known it's your birthday.

TOM. Connor loved London. Especially the red buses. We went to the Tower of London one year. Actually, we never got in, because we spent the whole day on buses because of the Lord Mayor's Show and when we finally did get there it was closed.

CONNOR. That was the best birthday ever, Mum. Mum, did you hear me?

SARA. I'm glad.

TOM. Connor really enjoyed the little things in life.

ROSIE. He could be dead fussy. But easy to please if you got it right.

SARA. There was his favourite shop in Holborn.

CONNOR. I love it here, Mum. I love it.

SARA. It sold these incredibly expensive models of buses and coaches. Connor would choose one and then stand by the cash desk after I paid for it, open the packaging, and very carefully, very deliberately, snap off the wing mirrors.

CONNOR (*snapping one*). That's better.

SARA. The staff couldn't believe it. And then we'd go and have lunch in Chinatown. He'd eat crispy duck, drink a Coke, and carefully park his new bus on the table in front of him. And we'd eat in silence. Bliss. Total bliss.


**1.8**

CONNOR. Mum.

SARA. Yes?

CONNOR. Is Chunky Stan dead?

SARA. He is, matey. He died just after Christmas.

CONNOR. Why, Mum?

SARA. He was very old, and the vet put him down.

CONNOR. Did the vet put him down, Mum?

SARA. She did.

CONNOR. Why, Mum?

SARA. Because he was very uncomfortable, and she thought it was kinder. We agreed.

CONNOR. Why, Mum?

SARA. Because he was so old.

CONNOR. Am *I* dead, Mum?

SARA. Yes.

CONNOR. And am I old, Mum?

SARA. No.

CONNOR. So why did I die, Mum?

SARA. Because –

*Pause.*

Because you were never given the chance.

## 1.9

ROSIE. I tell you what's hard. When someone like Connor turns eighteen. There's all this jargon. People 'transition to adult services'. Then they face 'dropping off the cliff edge'. Yep, that's right: 'The cliff edge.' And suddenly everything changes.

SARA. His social worker had planned to visit him at school to consider his next steps.

ROSIE. In his 'setting', as they call it. Which he attends with his 'peers'.

SARA. She came to see me at home first. Coffee or tea?

SOCIAL WORKER. Oh, tea please, one sugar. By the way, Mrs Ryan, I'm afraid I won't be able to visit your son this afternoon. I have to be in the office, you see. I have a couple of very important meetings and –

SARA. No worries. He didn't want to see you anyway.

SOCIAL WORKER. Well, he should. I am his future.

SARA. I was so angry I could have –

RICH. But thankfully she didn't.

SARA. Actually, Connor had very clear ideas about his future. Didn't you, matey?

CONNOR. Yeah, I want to own a lorry company. I'm gonna call it ConnorCo, and I'm gonna marry a beautiful girl with big brown eyes and long dark hair and we'll live happily ever after.

SARA. I'm afraid having a job isn't often heard in 'transition'.

ROSIE. 'The cliff edge'.

SARA. Which begs the question, 'transition' to what?

ROSIE. Since only a handful of adults with learning disabilities are in work, you'd think it would be a hot topic.

SARA. But instead, people like Connor are treated as expensive bundles of trouble. No ambition for them. No imagination.

CONNOR. But I liked Helen House, didn't I, Mum? Cool interview, wasn't it, Mum? I took the bus, didn't I, Mum? I got the job, didn't I, Mum?

SARA. You did, matey, and you did brilliantly. And a job as a groundsman at Helen House Children's Hospice would have been fantastic. Absolutely fantastic.

CONNOR. But I never started there, did I, Mum?

SARA. No, you didn't. You were admitted to the Unit a month later, before we'd sorted out the paperwork. Before –

## 1.10

RICH. Near the end of 2012. Connor went on a school trip to Devon and he threatened to attack a young teaching assistant.

CONNOR. He nicked my bloody toolkit. Wanker.

RICH. So, I picked him up in the car. He was completely unrecognisable.

CONNOR. Wankers.

RICH. Unreachable.

SARA. You can't imagine the sleepless nights. The endless worry.

RICH. And in early 2013 he often didn't get into school at all. He was too unpredictable. A real handful. We couldn't leave him with other people: he was a big lad now and he'd spend his days with his toolkit saying he was fixing the loo under the stairs.

CONNOR (*muttering*). Fuck off, wankers. Leave me alone. Leave me –

RICH. In March he punched his support teacher in the face. He loved Big Sue, but he punched her smack in the face.

CONNOR (*miming, with Big Sue*). Bang.

ROSIE. She was okay, but it wasn't great.

SARA. So sorry, Sue.

BIG SUE. Yeah, well, bit of a bruise, but I'll survive. He's a good lad.

RICH. And he got suspended.

SARA. Connor was in a really terrible way now. And he was six feet tall. Really strong.

*With a roar* CONNOR *suddenly threatens* SARA, *pushing her against a chair.*

Connor, stop it! Please.

Oh shit.

He had a spanner in his hand, and I had to leave the house and wait outside. I could hear him hurling himself against the bannisters upstairs.

I tried to get help. But all I heard from a psychiatrist was –

PSYCHIATRIST. I'm afraid he isn't my patient so I really can't offer much of an opinion. Why don't you talk to your GP?

GP 2. I can prescribe Lorazepam, if you like. It's a powerful sedative.

SARA. It knocked him out for most of the weekend. But we were 'a family in crisis'. We were in hell.

ROSIE. Mum, he's completely out.

SARA. Oh Christ, he looks awful.

Naively, I presumed that, come Monday, Social Care would come riding to the rescue. I phoned the psychiatric crisis line again.

PSYCHIATRIST'S SECRETARY. There's no record of your call, I'm afraid, Mrs, erm, I'll ask the doctor to call you later. What was the name?

SARA. Ryan, Sara Ryan.

PSYCHIATRIST'S SECRETARY. He's very busy, but I'm sure –

SARA. I rang every number on the list his social worker had given me.

ANOTHER RECEPTIONIST. Family members don't usually ring us direct, you know, our services are commissioned by Social Care, so it's not really for parents. I'm sorry not to be more helpful.

SARA. Well, fuck it, fuck it, fuck it.

*Pause.*

And then the phone rang.

*Phone rings.*

The truth is, I wish I'd never answered it.

I wish –

*Phone rings.*

Hello.

FRAN. Oh, hi Sara, it's Fran.

SARA. Oh, hello.

Fran was one of my best friends. Still is, actually.

FRAN. Look, Sara, I've just discovered that there's an Assessment and Treatment Unit in Oxford, an ATU they call them, and it's really near you, just off the ring road opposite the B&Q. It's called Slade House and apparently they've got really good staff – psychiatrists, OTs, autism specialists, the lot – and I'm sure they'll be able to work out why Connor is so – well, upset. It would just be for a few weeks. Why don't you give them a call?

SARA. Sounds great. I'll, erm –

FRAN. Do.

*Pause.*

It's run by Southern Health, Sara, so it's part of the NHS. And he'll still be able to go to school, so nothing will really change. I'll text you the phone number, I hope it helps –

SARA. Thanks, Fran. See you next week.

God, I hate this. Am I accepting that I can't cope? That I can't look after my own son? Am I really thinking about sending him away?

And he was *really* distressed now. That morning, two of his teaching assistants turned up to take him into town despite him being suspended. But even they had to bring him home early because they couldn't cope. So maybe this was the best option. Maybe –

*Dials.*

Oh, hello, yes, my name's, erm, Sara Ryan, yes, Dr Ryan, and I'd like to talk to you about my son – His name's Connor Sparrowhawk. S–P–A... Yes, it's a different name to mine, he's, erm –

*Pause.*

Yes, yes, he's –

*Pause.*

Great, thanks.

*Pause.*

That afternoon an on-call psychiatrist came round and talked to Connor for about five minutes and then longer to us, made a phone call, and told us Connor would be admitted that evening.

And so off we went. Into the dark.

RICH. Pretty shabby, isn't it? Like a barracks or something.

CONNOR. Can't see a thing, Mum.

SARA. It'll be alright, love, don't worry. Come on, guys. Let's get out of the car –

CONNOR. Weird, Mum.

SLADE HOUSE STAFF MEMBER 1. Oh hello?

SARA. Oh, hi, I'm Sara Ryan. This is Connor. And this is –

SLADE HOUSE STAFF MEMBER 1. Have you got an appointment?

SARA. Yes, Dr Johnson said we should come by at eight, so my son could be 'clerked in'. It's ten to, I think, isn't it?

RICH. It is.

SLADE HOUSE STAFF MEMBER 1. Right, well, you'd better, erm, go and wait in there, I suppose, and I'll try to find out what's going on.

SARA. Thanks.

You okay?

CONNOR *looks around grimly.*

They call this the 'living space'. A couple of battered sofas and an ancient TV with a plastic cover. Pale-green peeling paintwork. A stained brown carpet. And a polystyrene cup with cold tea in it sitting on the floor.

*Pause.*

And an hour later Rich and I left him there. That's right, we left him. All alone. In the dark.

*Pause.*

And I still can't believe it. I still can't –

TOM. And in the early hours of the morning he was forcibly restrained after he'd attacked a support worker.

SARA. Pinned face down to the floor by four adult males –

CONNOR (*struggling*). Get off me, you wankers, get off!

STAFF MEMBER. Steady on, laddie, play nicely.

SARA. And sectioned under the Mental Health Act. For twenty-eight days.

RICH. That was the night Connor left school forever.

SARA. That was the night his childhood ended.


## 1.11

ROSIE. So what do you imagine an Assessment and Treatment Unit does? The clue should be in the name.

SARA. But at Slade House, despite loads of specialist staff and one-to-one support – three and a half thousand quid a week each, if you please – there was bugger-all assessment or treatment going on. Just Risperidone tablets, 'to calm the lad down'.

ROSIE. He was drugged up to the eyes.

SLADE HOUSE STAFF MEMBER 2. And every Monday a ten-minute meeting –

SARA. Except on bank holidays, of course.

SLADE HOUSE STAFF MEMBER 2. – to discuss every patient.

CONNOR. Just leave me alone. Go away.

SARA. They told us that he'd be properly assessed. But although Dr Murphy, the clinician responsible, had an office across the car park, she didn't bother to visit him the next day, or the rest of the week, and on Saturday she went off on a two-week holiday. There was no ward round, no crisis intervention, no information, no nothing.

ROSIE. But incredibly tight controls over who could visit him, and when.

TOM. I couldn't go because I was thirteen. Too young to visit my own brother, apparently. So, one day Mum and I made a plan.

SARA. Burger King.

TOM. And I bought him a DVD. *21 Jump Street*. Where is he, Mum?

SARA. Dunno.

*On phone.*

Oh hi there, it's Connor's mother.

SLADE HOUSE STAFF MEMBER 1. Oh hello.

SARA. I'm here with Tom, Connor's younger brother. You were going to bring him down to meet us at six? Remember?

SLADE HOUSE STAFF MEMBER 1. Oh really? Can you hang on, Mum, while I check the board?

SARA. An interminable pause.

SLADE HOUSE STAFF MEMBER 1. Oh, sorry, Mum. We forgot. He's just finished his tea.

TOM. What?

SARA. And forty-five minutes later they brought him down. To see his own brother. He looked awful: haggard and tired.

RICH. One of the challenges of when a kid like Connor turns eighteen, is that he can choose to do whatever he likes.

SLADE HOUSE STAFF MEMBER 2. And because he's eighteen, you have to ring the Unit first if you want to visit him.

SARA. But what if he says he doesn't want us to visit?

SLADE HOUSE STAFF MEMBER 2. Well, that's his choice, I'm afraid.

SARA. And what if he says he wants us to visit him but no one answers the door? As has happened. What then?

SLADE HOUSE STAFF MEMBER 2. Oh, that's just weekends and bank holidays. Quite reasonable, really. Our staff work very hard, you know, and the patients can be very challenging, and we have to do what we can to protect staff morale. It's a question of –

SLADE HOUSE STAFF MEMBER 1. Limited resources.

SLADE HOUSE STAFF MEMBER 2. Staff overstretch.

SLADE HOUSE STAFF MEMBER 1. Tight budgets.

SLADE HOUSE STAFF MEMBER 2. But we do want to help, Mum. Really, we do. Choice is important to us.

SARA. Yeah, choice is important. But what are the choices available? Nothing. It's all just talk.

### 1.12

RICH. And then on 20 May 2013, six weeks before he died –

SARA. I found him on his bed, totally out of it.

*Pause.*

You alright, matey?

CONNOR. Uh?

SARA. What's up?

CONNOR. Mum, I –

SARA. What?

*Pause.*

He'd bitten his tongue and had obviously had a seizure. But in her wisdom, Dr Murphy had prescribed Bonjela. Yeah, that stuff you put on babies' gums when they're teething. Didn't you?

DR MURPHY. It was the right thing to do.

SARA. The fact is either she didn't consider the possibility of an epileptic seizure or decided against it without recording her reasons. Even though there was clear documentation about his sensitivity to changes in medication, which she'd recently introduced. Hadn't you?

DR MURPHY. Rightly so.

SARA. So later that evening I rang the Unit. Oh hello, it's Connor's mum. You do know, don't you, that Connor had a seizure earlier?

CHERYL. Sorry, who's this?

SARA. Connor's mum. He's had a, I'm sure he has. A seizure.

CHERYL. A what?

SARA. You know, an epileptic seizure?

CHERYL. Oh right. Yes, I'll, erm, pass that on, I'm just a student, you see, I erm –

SARA. Thank you. Please do. Jesus Christ.

*Pause.*

The idea of him having a seizure, in a locked unit, unnoticed, was the worst thing I could imagine.

At that point.

## 1.13

RICH. On ninth June we took Connor on a trip to London. He looked terrible. And on the way back he started hitting himself in the face.

CONNOR *does so*.

SARA. Matey, don't do that, really.

TOM. Connor, please don't.

CONNOR (*does it again*). Wankers. Wankers.

SARA. Matey –

CONNOR (*still hitting himself*). Fucking wankers.

TOM (*wrestling with him*). Connor, stop it, mate. Stop it. Mum, he's got a nosebleed.

SARA. He didn't want to go back. He really didn't.

CONNOR (*flipping a finger*). Fuck 'em. Fuck 'em. Fuck 'em. Wankers!

SARA. Oh love.

RICH. Meanwhile, the endless meetings went on.

SLADE HOUSE STAFF MEMBER 4. 'Minutes of the meeting to discuss and assess Connor Sparrowhawk's health and social care needs.'

SLADE HOUSE STAFF MEMBER 3. 'Mum said she was confused that CS had been admitted to the Unit for assessment and treatment, and asked where the assessment and the treatment was? Dr Murphy explained that CS is – '

DR MURPHY. 'Not our usual type of patient.'

SLADE HOUSE STAFF MEMBER 3. 'He's in transition, and younger than most. Working with school is unusual.'

SARA. So that's okay then, is it?

Meanwhile, now that the Section had ended, Social Care started talking about a possible provision to be decided at some unspecified meeting in the nearish future. More blah.

ROSIE. And where would he go? Some godawful place where he'd sit around all day eating junk food, watching daytime TV and rotting.

SARA. I visited one day and his room had been painted. All the stuff he'd stuck up on the walls over the last few months were piled up in the corner. He was kneeling on the floor, flicking through a truck magazine. Surrounded by empty white walls and nothingness.

CONNOR. I want to go home, Mum. Mum, can I go home?

SARA. We're trying to sort things out, matey. Promise.

RICH. The next day Sara sent an email apologising for being unable to attend that morning's meeting, adding that Connor 'seems quite apathetic and not very responsive'. Did the staff agree?

SLADE HOUSE STAFF MEMBER 1. Mum's concerns were raised and dismissed.

SARA. The truth is the weekend staff saw that he was out of it, but no one on the Monday bothered to read the notes. And the next day I took my parents to visit him. It was the last time I saw him alive.


## 1.14

RICH. Fourth July 2013. The relatives' room at the John Radcliffe Hospital. Simple modern furniture. A couple of prints on the wall. A view through a small window of a blank brick wall. The agony this room must have known.

CONSULTANT. I'm sorry, Mrs Ryan, but this is serious. Your son is on a ventilator in the, erm – Just through here.

SARA. And he explained to me calmly and clearly that they wanted my permission to turn off the machine. That's right, isn't it? Turn off the machine?

CONSULTANT. I'm afraid so. There's nothing we can do.

*Pause.*

SARA. Yes, do it. Thank you.

*Long pause.*

Rosie, Rich and I went in to see him later.

ROSIE. Hi, Connor.

RICH. Hey.

SARA. Matey.

*Pause.*

I, erm –

*Pause.*

What are you meant to say?

ORGAN DONOR NURSE. Forgive me, Mrs Ryan, but could I just –

SARA. And quick as a flash Connor's heart valves were taken from him. Brutal, isn't it? But I like to think some young person somewhere has caught some of his magic.

And then we went home. I don't know how, but we did. We left him alone in the hospital and we went home. My laughing boy. My beautiful laughing boy.

EVERYBODY *sings the bridge of 'It's a Wonderful Life' going into verse three.*

*Cuts off suddenly.*

**PART TWO: AFTER**

**2.1**

SARA. One day Connor was completely alive.

The next day completely dead.

*Pause.*

And now a house full of flowers. Hugs, kindness and too much booze. And I sometimes forget that it ever happened. But then it all comes crashing in again.

*Pause.*

I spent hours in the garden staring at the sky, late into the night, searching for something, some sort of way of making sense of what had happened, weeping or walking in the park with the dogs.

*Pause.*

Connor was dead. Connor is dead. Connor will always be dead. How is that possible, how can – ?

RICH. Love, this is Mr Jeffs, and erm –

FUNERAL DIRECTOR. I know this is terribly painful, madam, and my condolences, but I do need to ask whether you'd prefer burial or cremation?

SARA. What?

FUNERAL DIRECTOR. Burial or cremation for your – ?

SARA. I don't want either. Stop this. Now.

FUNERAL DIRECTOR. I'm sorry, madam, but I do need a decision. If you want a burial, we'll have to find a plot. The Oxford cemeteries –

SARA. Look, my son is eighteen. He was getting ready to visit the Oxford Bus Company. He. Can't. Be. Cremated. Okay?

FUNERAL DIRECTOR. Let me see what can be done.

RICH. Thank you.

SARA. And that's what happened. They found a place for him. That's right, a grave. And two weeks later we buried my eighteen-year-old son. In a grave.

RICH. We'll show you later.

If we can bear it.


## 2.2

SARA. So, what now? How do you pick yourself up from that? We could just have accepted the explanation and tried to carry on. Stumbling forward, numb with tears.

RICH. Maybe that would have been easier.

*Pause.*

SARA. But then something extraordinary happened. I posted a simple one-line Tweet saying that Connor had died, and within a few hours a human rights barrister contacted me out of the blue and offered to help. Meet Caoilfhionn Gallagher. A force of nature.

CAOILFHIONN GALLAGHER (*on phone*). Look, Sara, I'm afraid you should be prepared for the possibility that Connor's death isn't properly investigated. There's a great charity called INQUEST which offers free advice.

SARA. So I spoke to someone there who said we needed a solicitor.

CHARLOTTE HAWORTH HIRD. Hello, Dr Ryan. Now, look, the crucial first step is to establish whether the pathologist conducted his post-mortem using the standard guidelines for epilepsy. It's grim, I know, but essential. Their statement of 'unascertained death' just isn't good enough. Do you think you could call him?

SARA. Did I have the courage?

TOM. It was my fourteenth birthday and Mum took me into town to get me a present.

SARA. And passing by the funeral home I suddenly realised that Connor would have been stark naked when they hauled him off to hospital. And he must have been naked when I turned the machine off.

So that evening we picked up some of his clothes and went in to see him: his favourite onesie, a cool T-shirt, socks, his new trainers. I claimed my boy back. In the funeral home. For just a moment.

*Pause.*

And the next day I made the call. I was in the back garden. It was so hot. I remember staring at a pebbledash wall. Sweating like a pig.

PATHOLOGIST (*defensive, vague, on the phone*). Yes, I'm pretty certain I did. As far as I can remember. But they're just 'guidelines', you know, Mrs Ryan, brain tissue of people with epilepsy isn't routinely sampled, because it rarely reveals anything of consequence. It's terribly complicated and, erm –

SARA. And a huge part of me wanted to stick my head under the duvet and cry.

CHARLOTTE HAWORTH HIRD. I do understand, Sara, but I'm going to be brutal. You must be able to make an informed decision.

SARA. What d'you mean?

CHARLOTTE HAWORTH HIRD. Well, Connor's body needs to be taken back to the hospital for one last test. We need to get a proper sample of his brain tissue.

SARA. Oh Christ.

*Pause.*

But, yes, informed decision making. That's what we need, and it's so bloody rare. Thank you, Charlotte, thank you.

And I persuaded them to take his body back to the hospital and have another look.

**2.3**

RICH. Meanwhile –

SOUTHERN HEALTH TRUST. In March, we at Southern
Health became aware of a blog post written by Sara Ryan,
the deceased's mother. We decided to monitor it.

SARA. I'd started writing *My Daft Life* long before Connor
died. Just funny stuff about everyday life. Pictures. Stories.
Look.

*Projection.*

But more and more worries about Connor.

*Projection.*

This was my post the day he died.

*Projection.*

That's right.

SOUTHERN HEALTH TRUST. This blog mentioned several
staff members by name and is, we believe, defamatory.

RICH. Later we saw a document published by Southern Health
the day after Connor's death.

SARA. Not a squeak about what I'd actually written, just a load
of stuff about their reputation. They were most concerned by
my post on twenty-first May, six weeks before he died.

TOM (*reading*). 'LB's seizures have always worried the pants
off me. Not least because it took about four in-your-face
tonic-clonics before the doctors would even consider that he
had epilepsy.'

ROSIE (*reading*). 'The thought of him having a seizure in
a locked unit unnoticed has generated a new level of distress
I can't describe. I don't care how old he is, and I'm certainly
not treating him like a child, but I want to comfort him, and
keep a watchful eye for any further seizures. And I can't.'

SARA. That says it all, really, doesn't it? I can't keep a watchful eye over him. I can't protect him. I can't and I couldn't. So maybe I'm to blame. Maybe I shouldn't have worried about him. Maybe I shouldn't have questioned what they were doing. Maybe I should have kept my big mouth shut.

Maybe.

## 2.4

ROSIE. And six long weeks after Connor's death the CQC finally got round to inspecting the Unit.

SARA. We knew it was shite, but the report showed it was much, much worse than we'd imagined.

CQC 1. Hardly any social or therapeutic interactions.

CQC 2. Medicines inadequately administered.

CQC 3. Emergency oxygen significantly out of date.

CQC 2. A defibrillator with no battery inside.

CQC 4. And human faeces in a drawer.

SARA. Sweet Jesus.

SOUTHERN HEALTH TRUST. In our defence Southern Health was stopped by the police from discovering what had been going on and we accepted the reassurances given us by our first-class staff.

RICH. That bloody dog of ours must have eaten their homework.

CONNOR (*with Stan*). Stan, come on, Stan!

RICH. Don't let him lick your face, matey!

CONNOR *barks like Stan*.

SARA (*laughing*). Connor!

We soon heard that the county council had expressed concern, a while back, about the physical state of Slade

House, the lack of proper care plans and the limited evidence of, you guessed it, assessment or treatment. All of which were ignored.

RICH. And two months later, Mike Holder, an independent health and safety officer brought in to review the matter, had resigned in protest.

MIKE HOLDER. The truth is health and safety was treated as an add-on to the Trust's core business. When I expressed my concerns they insisted that they had to tolerate a certain degree of risk. I pointed out that it had an absolute duty to ensure the safety of its patients, particularly the most vulnerable.

SARA. Hear that? An absolute duty. Which it absolutely failed to deliver.

ROSIE, TOM, WILL *and* OWEN. That's what killed our brother.

SARA *and* RICH. And that's what killed our son.


## 2.5

RICH. As a result of all this Sara started to call Southern Health 'Sloven'.

SARA. Seemed a perfect nickname.

*Projection.*

'Slovenly sloven.'

RICH. And reading the board papers for a Trust meeting about Connor just a fortnight after his death, Sara came across this:

SOUTHERN HEALTH TRUST (*reading*). 'A Serious Incident Requiring Investigation occurred in one of the Trust's learning disability inpatient facilities, leading to the unexpected death of a service user.'

SARA. 'The unexpected death of a service user'?!

SOUTHERN HEALTH TRUST. 'The post-mortem indicates the user died of natural causes and early investigations indicate all appropriate systems and processes were in place and being followed leading up to the incident. A full investigation is underway. Support has been offered to his family and the staff.'

ROSIE. What do they mean by 'natural causes', Mum?

SARA. I've no idea.

ROSIE. And why do they say his death was 'unexpected'?

SARA. I don't know.

ROSIE. Why would they write that in their board papers?

SARA. Not a clue.

ROSIE. It doesn't make any sense, does it, Mum?

SARA. No, Rosie, it doesn't.

### 2.6

RICH. What were we meant to do with this pain? All of us, I mean.

SARA. Well, among his many talents, Connor had a fierce sense of justice. Come on, matey, empty the bloody dishwasher for a change.

CONNOR. That's not fair, Mum, I'm calling my lawyer, you know what human rights are, don't you, Mum? I need my lawyer, I'm going to call my –

SARA. So, he got a lawyer. In fact, he got more than a lawyer, he got a whole bloody campaign. The least he deserved.

RICH. And then, suddenly – surprise, surprise – four months after his death, Sloven announced an internal investigation into what had happened.

SARA. Apparently, it's going to take four weeks and will be headed up by the same bloke who did their review back in November 2012.

ROSIE. How does that work?

SARA. I've no idea, love. I suspect he'll go in, poke about a bit, cut and paste some nice warm words, and circulate it to everyone involved. Move along now. Nothing to see.

ROSIE. But Connor died, Mum. There has to be an independent investigation. There has to be.

SARA. Exactly.


## 2.7

RICH. It soon became obvious, even to Sloven, that this wasn't good enough, and so they appointed a team of independent consultants called Verita.

ROSIE. It means 'the truth'. Apparently.

SARA. Their report was due on 24 February 2014. By this time a whole gang of people had gathered round the campaign. Team LB, we called ourselves. Meet George Julian, campaigner. Fighter for justice.

GEORGE JULIAN. I knew Sloven would mess us around with publishing the report online. On the day it was due, they kept us waiting all day: more evidence, if needed, of the contempt they showed Connor and his family. But Twitter doesn't close at 6 p.m., which is when the thing finally came out.

SARA. Bloody hell, it's sixty pages long.

GEORGE JULIAN. Loads of names redacted. And twenty-three findings, including:

ROSIE. 'No evidence that an epilepsy profile was completed.'

OWEN. 'No proper care plan to manage his epilepsy.'

TOM. 'No increase in monitoring after a suspected seizure.'

RICH. 'No evidence that he'd been observed in the bath every fifteen minutes.'

ROSIE. And look, only three of the seventeen members of staff had had up-to-date epilepsy training.

GEORGE JULIAN. Poor Connor didn't stand a chance. The
   level of care was negligible. His death was completely
   preventable. It was obvious to everyone.

SARA. But as I read on something made me pause.

*Pause.*

The report said the idea that Connor had had a seizure in
May was dismissed by the clinical team. They said he'd
bitten his tongue because he was in a bad mood. But no one
had told *us*. And I realised that his statement – from the boy
who *always* denied he had epilepsy – had been taken as firm
evidence that he'd not had a seizure.

*Pause.*

Why would anyone rule out seizures in a young man with
diagnosed epilepsy? And what I didn't ask at the time is, why
did Dr Murphy, yes you, Dr Murphy –

DR MURPHY. Oh, hello.

SARA. Why did you make the decision to reduce his
   observations to hourly, claiming that there was 'no evidence'
   of seizure activity? It's not good enough, is it?

RICH. The report missed this, and justice hadn't been done.

*Pause.*

Luckily, the inquest loomed.


## 2.8

NORMAN LAMB MP. Oh, good evening, everyone, I'm
   Norman Lamb. I'd been an MP since 2001 and was Minister
   for Community and Social Care. I met Sara at a social-care
   curry night and after some confusion – probably my fault –
   she told me what had happened. I promised to do whatever
   I could. How could I not?

SARA. Thank you.

RICH. And then we had a meeting with David Nicholson, the head of NHS England. We then banged out the Connor Manifesto, an attempt to describe what a whole bunch of us wanted to happen, not just in relation to Connor, but other people with learning disabilities. And then we had a meeting with David Nicholson, the head of NHS England.

SARA. And Nicholson, who was about to retire, agreed to, quote, 'commission an investigation into the deaths of all patients with learning disabilities in the Southern Health Foundation Trust between 2011 and 2015'.

RICH. The results were utterly brutal. More soon.

## 2.9

SARA. And then, something utterly magical happened.

TOM. We decided to mark the year since Connor had gone into Slade House –

ROSIE. By asking all sorts of people to adopt one of the one hundred and seven days he spent there. In any way they liked. They did everything. You name it. The creativity was amazing.

TOM. Just look at this:

## Intermezzo

*Loud music and projections counting up the 107 days. Tweets, images, voices, statements, etc. (See the catalogue on pp. 252– 269 of* Justice for Laughing Boy.)

*Sudden silence after 106.*

## 2.10

SARA. Culminating with the first anniversary of –

*Pause.*

GEORGE JULIAN. We didn't know what to do, so we asked everyone to change their Twitter profile to this.

*Projection.*

See?

CONNOR. Wow, Mum.

SARA. So many people got involved. Dedicated. Creative. Funny people.

*Pause. Laughs.*

Fucking sweary.

*Pause.*

And always kind.

*Pause.*

See what you started, matey?

CONNOR. A campaign, Mum?

SARA. Yes, matey. An amazing, amazing campaign.

CONNOR. Mum, Mum, is there a play about me, Mum? Is it in London, Mum? Does it have buses in it, Mum?

SARA. Yes. And yes it does. And so much more.

CONNOR. Cool.

ROSIE. Loads of people were working for free, but we needed some dosh: twenty grand, in fact, for legal costs.

TOM. So we did loads of crazy things. We even printed postcards of Connor's artwork and sold them online for a quid each.

RICH. We'll get there eventually, guys.

TOM. And we did.

CONNOR. Twenty grand? Fucking hell.

TOM. Yeah, well, you deserve it, bro.

ROSIE. So much magic. So much love.

TOM. So much laughter. So much hard work.

SARA. So much rage. And so many tears.

*Pause.*

But it took its toll. On all of us. And the kids were still so young.

## 2.11

RICH. Meet Mary-Ann Bruce.

MARY-ANN BRUCE. Hello, I'm the Director of the Health Advisory team at the consultancy firm Mazar's, and David Nicholson from the NHS has asked me to lead an investigation into deaths within Southern Health learning disability and mental-health services. We invited Sara Ryan and her husband onto the steering group.

SARA. Morning.

RICH. Is that – ? I'm sorry but you can't have someone from the Trust on the steering group. You really can't.

SARA. I don't blame him. I managed to stay put. Just.

MARY-ANN BRUCE. The meeting was quickly over. The person from Southern Health was taken off the steering group and two lay members added.

RICH. See? You have to keep your eyes open and be an awkward bugger.

SARA. Because if you don't –

RICH. Well, they win. And that's the truth.

*Pause.*

SARA. But what really hurts are the anniversaries. Christmas. His birthday. His death day. We do what we can.

RICH. Our house is full of Connor stuff. Paintings, photos, memories. Every mantelpiece and bookcase. Every wall.

ROSIE. Buses everywhere. So many buses!

CONNOR. Yeah, well, I loved buses, didn't I, Mum?

SARA. You did, matey. And coaches.

CONNOR. And coaches, Mum. Yeah, I loved coaches. And buses.

RICH. And this is what he was wearing when we buried him:

ROSIE. His Sebastien Bonaparte T-shirt.

TOM. His mechanics overalls.

ROSIE. The trainers Mum bought him a few weeks before he died.

RICH. And he had with him:

ROSIE. His first-aid book.

TOM. A load of model buses and trucks.

RICH. Septic tank ads torn out of the Yellow Pages.

TOM. Pictures of friends and family.

SARA. And a photo of –

ROSIE. His mum.

SARA. What a dude, eh? What a dude.

*Pause.*

So why are we telling you all this?

*Pause.*

Well, it should be obvious.

*Pause.*

But maybe it isn't. And not everyone gets this. But the fact is, you see, whatever his differences, whatever his so-called disabilities, Connor was a human being, just like you and me, just like all of us. And too often that gets forgotten.

*Pause.*

But that's what we're fighting for. The right of people like my Connor, our Connor, to be treated as human beings. Human rights, not human problems.

*Pause.*

It's not that hard, is it?

*It gets darker.*

TOM. This is from Mum's blog, about eight weeks after Connor died.

'Bit of a tough twenty-four hours really. Starting with an unannounced unexpected lengthy weep fest yesterday evening.'

ROSIE (*reading*). 'I'm not sure I was even crying really. Well, not in any way I'd ever experienced before. And, boy, we're talking some serious crying in the last two months. The Lynx deodorant smells have almost gone. But his odour clings on.'

SARA. Dismantling his room was tough, to put it mildly. Friends helped. Friends do.


**2.12**

TOM. It's time to tell you about the Justice Quilt. Meet Janet Read.

JANET READ. Oh, hello, everyone. So, my idea for Day fifty-ninewas to make an enormous patchwork quilt. So, we asked everyone we could think of to come up with little square patches, this big, and we sewed them all together.

Look.

*Projection of the quilt.*

We wanted something big and bright and colourful, to express the many different people working together on a single, beautiful cause.

Look how gorgeous these are. So much love. So much care.

*Projections of a series of individual patches.*

TOM. And, surprise, surprise, loads of London buses.

*Projections of patches with buses.*

ROSIE. Other things too, all individual, all linked. Hearts, hands, and the simplest of questions –

*Projections of others asking 'Why?'*

JANET READ. Why?

EVERYONE (*echoing and repeating*). Why?

JANET READ. A beautiful quilt to keep you warm in a cold, desperate world.

**PART THREE: JUSTICE**

**3.1**

SARA. Your inquest was seven years ago, LB. You would have loved it.

CONNOR. Was there a judge, Mum?

SARA. A Coroner, that's a type of judge. And a jury.

CONNOR. How many people, Mum?

SARA. Nine. And eight legal teams, loads of barristers and solicitors. Yours were the best.

CONNOR. Barristers and solicitors, Mum?

SARA. Yep.

CONNOR. And did lots of people give evidence, Mum?

SARA. They did.

CONNOR. Did they swear on oath, Mum?

SARA. Everyone did.

CONNOR. On the Bible, Mum?

SARA. Or some sort of affirmation thingy.

CONNOR. And what did the Coroner say, Mum?

SARA. He said –

*Pause.*

– he said he was sorry you died.

CONNOR. Is that all?

SARA. He was *very* sorry you died.

**3.2**

CORONER. Morning, everyone. I'm Darren Salter, Her
Majesty's Senior Coroner for Oxford. I must declare
from the outset that the state had a duty to protect Connor
Sparrowhawk's life because, at the time of his death, he was
in the care of the NHS. Since that duty was breached, he's
entitled to what we call an Article 2 Inquest.

CORONER. And, under certain circumstances, such an inquest
can necessitate a jury.

SARA. Good.

CAOILFHIONN GALLAGHER. Look, Sara, I've just seen
a submission from Southern Health's lawyers who say that
the obligation to investigate Connor's death has already been
met – by the police, the Health and Safety Executive, NHS
England and the Care Quality Commission. And so they're
arguing that an Article 2 Inquest isn't necessary. They also
say there's no need for a jury –

SARA. You're joking.

CAOILFHIONN GALLAGHER. – because, while, quote, 'the
deceased died in state detention, it can't be said that, one, the
death was violent or unnatural or, two, that the cause of death
is unknown'.

SARA. Drowning in an NHS bath is natural?

CAOILFHIONN GALLAGHER. They're encouraging the
Coroner to, quote, 'think independently'.

SARA. What does that mean?

CAOILFHIONN GALLAGHER. They also say that while the
family's views are important, they, quote, are not wholly
determinate of the matter.

SARA. They're shitting on us again, aren't they? From a great
height.

*Pause.*

So what do we do?

CAOILFHIONN GALLAGHER. We keep on fighting.

CORONER. Ladies and gentlemen, your attention please. It's clear to me that the argument that Connor Sparrowhawk died as a result of natural causes is unsound and, following this interesting debate, the Article 2 Inquest will go ahead.

SARA. Finally.

CORONER. But I will not empanel a jury. Connor was not in custody or state detention and was therefore at liberty to leave the Unit.

SARA. With respect, you didn't know Connor. How can you say that?

CORONER. Mrs Ryan, if your son had asked for the front door to be unlocked the staff would have unlocked it. He was hardly detained.

SARA. But he would never have asked for the door to be unlocked. And even if every door had been unlocked, he wouldn't have left the Unit alone. He didn't open the door to me years ago when I locked myself out of the house. And everyone on the Unit knew he wanted to come home.

CORONER. One moment, please.

SARA. Fingers crossed.

*Pause.*

CORONER. I agree to empanel a jury.

SARA. Thank fuck.

CAOILFHIONN GALLAGHER. You see, Sloven knew juries are sceptical of authority and so they were desperate to block one. We badly needed one.


**3.3**

RICH. Sara was knackered.

SARA. And we were only just beginning.

RICH. So then came the final pre-inquest hearing.

SOUTHERN HEALTH LAWYER. Good morning, I'm here
to represent Southern Health and we have three procedural
concerns. First, it's inappropriate for Richard Huggins, Mrs
Ryan's, erm, partner, to give evidence. After all, he's not the
deceased's father and has no legal status in relationship to
him. Second, Mrs Ryan should give oral evidence only once,
at the start of proceedings. And third, the Court must exclude
jurors who've read or been exposed to Mrs Ryan's blog.

CORONER. I'm afraid you're going to find that last point hard
to satisfy. It's terribly popular, you know.

SARA. You see, Sloven was desperate to do everything it could
to cut us out. I'd call that an attempted stitch-up.

What would you call it?

## PART FOUR: THE INQUEST, SET UP

**4.1**

RICH. It's October 2015 and the inquest itself is scheduled to last two weeks.

SARA. We had a great support team. Rosie and her partner. The lads. My parents and my sister. Friends and allies. And, of course, George Julian.

GEORGE JULIAN. I moved in. A camp bed in the downstairs back room. And I tweeted the whole damn thing. People needed to know what was going on.

SARA. How to describe the Coroners' Court? Let my mate John tell you. He's good at this sort of thing.

JOHN LISH (*acting this out*). New County Hall has a hidden entrance. The foyer's just a corridor, really. In front, closed doors, To your right, more closed doors. Finally, doors leading into the Court. This isn't a public space: it's a private space that grudgingly permits public engagement. The physical equivalent of what the Director of Social Care told Sara:

DIRECTOR OF SOCIAL CARE. Mrs Ryan, you do everything the wrong way round. We offered a private meeting, but you put your comments online. It doesn't work like that. Really, it doesn't.

**4.2**

JOHN LISH. The Coroner sits up there with his officer below. The press box is over on the left, the jury box is on the right. Rows of benches for the legal teams and a huge long table. Tall windows behind the jury box. Empty sky.

SARA. And then, matey, an A4 picture of you on the Coroner's desk, looking out.

CONNOR. Me, Mum?

SARA. Yep, you. And at the end of the first week, a different one. Lest they forget.

CONNOR. Not just a name, Mum, not just a name.

SARA. Exactly.

CORONER. Good morning, everyone. We will now resume the inquest into the death of Mr Connor Sparrowhawk. Now then, I must ask, have any of you read Mrs Ryan's blog, or any social-media comments about Southern Health?

*Pause.*

Well, don't.


## 4.3

RICH. There was this family room, down another corridor. At least we didn't have to be in the canteen with all the lawyers.

OWEN. We all hung out together.

WILL. McDonald's. Kebabs.

ROSIE. Eugh.

SARA. We tried to work out toilet trips, so we didn't bump into anyone. I remember once Dr Jayawant –

DR JAYAWANT (*mouthing*). Are. You. Okay?

SARA. I just ignored her.

RICH. Loads of people from the campaign turned up.

FRAN. Hi, it's Fran. Remember: I told Sara about Slade House in the first place.

Anyway, I was up in the public gallery. You wouldn't believe the bullshit the Trust came up with. My son's in their so-called care, but they don't really give a toss.

RICH. We calmed her down. Just. And then the whole thing got going.

### 4.4

SARA. You had the best lawyers, matey.

CONNOR. Did I, Mum?

SARA. The absolute best.

WILL. Paul Bowen, QC. The silver fox.

CONNOR. Cool, Mum.

PAUL BOWEN QC. So, look, Sara, their lawyers seem to have two lines of defence. The first is that, quote, 'there's no evidence Connor had seizure activity while in the Unit'. And the second is that they're going to discredit you.

SARA. Me?

PAUL BOWEN QC. 'Fraid so.

COUNSEL 1 (*overlapping voices*). There's absolutely no evidence of epilepsy while Connor was at home –

COUNSEL 2. We really should consider his mother's behaviour throughout –

COUNSEL 3. Consider Mrs Ryan's blog, the abuse on social media, all the dreadful name-calling –

COUNSEL 4. His mother has been consistently obstructive and difficult.

CONNOR. Wankers!

SARA. That's right, matey, wankers. Complete and utter wankers.

*Pause.*

They then played the calls between Dr Jayawant and 999.

RESPONDER. Ambulance. Is the patient breathing?

DR JAYAWANT. Oh, hello, we need an ambulance at Slade House, yes, the NHS Unit in Headington, as we have a patient here who I suspect has possibly had a seizure, no, he is not breathing. We don't know how long...

*The call starts to fade.*

SARA. I couldn't cope and got up and left.

CORONER. Nurse Dullaghan, did you at any stage carry out an assessment of Connor's physical needs with respect to his epilepsy and the risk around bathing?

COUNSEL 3. My client refuses to answer on the grounds of possible self-incrimination.

CORONER. I see.

SARA. But the next day Connor's other key nurse struck a different note.

WINNIE BETSVA. Can I say something? To the family?

CORONER. Of course.

WINNIE BETSVA. Well, I just want to say that I'm ever so sorry about what happened. I really am.

SARA. Thank you. It was the first time anyone had offered an apology.


**4.5**

RICH. The one thing the inquest never established was what exactly happened that morning.

SARA. And we still don't know. The only thing we do know is that Connor was going to have a bath before visiting the Oxford Bus Company. God, he loved the Oxford Bus Company.

CONNOR. I loved the Oxford Bus Company. Didn't I, Mum?

SARA. You did, matey. You did.

*Pause as she gathers herself.*

RICH. Anyway, according to the paperwork, his support worker and key worker were supposed to check in on him every fifteen minutes until 9.15 when –

KIERAN DULLAGHAN. Yeah, we were in the nurses' office just across the corridor.

CORONER. What sort of distance would that be?

KIERAN DULLAGHAN (*demonstrates*). This, maybe?

MAXINE HEMMINGS. I was doing an online Tesco order –

SARA. New potatoes or salad potatoes?

KIERAN DULLAGHAN. – between checking up on him.

SARA. While Connor drowned in the fucking bath?

MAXINE HEMMINGS. Yeah, Kieran did most of the checking.

KIERAN DULLAGHAN. You checked up on him a couple of times.

MAXINE HEMMINGS. I don't think I did. What d'you mean?

CORONER. Please tell us what happened when you found him.

MAXINE HEMMINGS. Well, I unlocked the bathroom door and –

CORONER. Excuse me?

SARA. What?

CORONER. Why was it locked?

KIERAN DULLAGHAN. Oh, we always lock the door when they're in the bath.

MAXINE HEMMINGS. So they can't, you know –

CORONER. What?

MAXINE HEMMINGS. Well, you know, run around the place naked.

KIERAN DULLAGHAN. Connor was a young lad. And you have to, well, let him do what young lads do in the bathroom. And female staff are –

SARA. Oh, for fuck's sake. Our downstairs bathroom doesn't have a door. We'd all wander in and out. Chat through the open door, 'Don't forget to wash your hair, Connor. Got to look cool tomorrow –'

CONNOR. Not gonna.

SARA. Even on school trips the teacher would stand outside the shower, even for kids who didn't have epilepsy. It's common sense.

CONNOR. Wankers!

SARA (*breaking down*). So, who checked, eh? Did you ever bother to check? Or did you suddenly think, oh God, where is he, and unlock the door and find him drowned in the bath? Didn't you hear the splashes? Tell me the truth, you bastards, tell me the –

RICH. We never got an answer.

*Pause.*

Actually, Sara never spoke like that. She didn't risk it. But it's how she felt.


### 4.6

SARA. And then there was the elusive Dr Murphy herself.

CORONER. I must ask you, Dr Murphy, and I realise how busy you were, but if you knew that Connor had had a seizure, would it have been appropriate to leave him alone in a bath?

DR MURPHY. As you know, and as was borne out by the initial investigation, my professional assessment was that Connor hadn't had a seizure on the 20th. Indeed, he himself said he remembered biting his tongue when he was angry.

CORONER. But you assessed him when he was on the Unit?

DR MURPHY. Yes, but that's not relevant to this line of inquiry.

CORONER. Perhaps, but let me ask you again: if you knew that Connor had had a seizure, would it have been appropriate to leave him alone in the bath?

DR MURPHY. If it was a proven seizure, no. But my clear understanding is that Connor didn't have a seizure while he was on the Unit.

CORONER. That's not really sustainable, is it, Dr Murphy, when we know that Connor had one on the day he died?

DR MURPHY. No comment.

CORONER. Thank you. Mr Bowen, you had some questions, I believe.

PAUL BOWEN QC. Thank you. Dr Murphy, I'm sure you'll agree that Dr Ryan had seen her son have seizures in the past?

DR MURPHY. Yes.

PAUL BOWEN QC. And that she'd seen how he presented afterwards?

DR MURPHY. Yes.

PAUL BOWEN QC. So, you'll also agree that she was the best person to know, having seen him that day, whether it was likely or not that he'd had a seizure.

DR MURPHY. Perhaps.

PAUL BOWEN QC. You'll have heard the expert witness of Professor Crawford, Consultant Neurologist and Director of the Epilepsy Centre in York, who draws the firm conclusion that Connor bit his tongue as a result of an unobserved seizure. Do you agree with her?

DR MURPHY. With respect, Professor Crawford wasn't there.

PAUL BOWEN QC. You weren't there either, were you, Dr Murphy?

DR MURPHY. No.

PAUL BOWEN QC. Thank you, that'll be all.

**4.7**

RICH. Of course, the person who was really to blame for Connor's death –

*Pause.*

SARA. Was me.

RICH. That's right. You.

SARA. A few months before the inquest, Charlotte sent me some witness statements.

CHARLOTTE. Concerning the staff's, quote, difficult relationship with Dr Ryan.

SARA. People I thought I'd got along with. Like this student nurse:

CHERYL. I'd seen Dr Ryan shouting at a consultant. I was terrified of her.

SARA. You see, when the shit hits the fan, they blame the mum: fuck knows why, but it's usually the mum.

Actually, it's something bigger: a complete failure to understand the families themselves. Just no interest at all.

RICH. And then we saw this letter from an Oxfordshire commissioner.

OXFORDSHIRE COMMISSIONER. 'I feel deep sympathy for Dr Ryan in her terrible loss but I'm afraid, in hindsight, her campaigning did a great deal of damage. Although I recognise that we could perhaps have done more, she really should acknowledge the enormous financial strains under which our services were operating. We're all very sorry for what happened but bloggers and commentators have a duty to be honest and accurate. My hope is that Dr Ryan can find some kind of peace and that one day she might be able to move on.'

SARA. Just like that, eh? Our campaign was damaging, eh, Rich? A campaign to –

*Pause.*

Thankfully, the student nurse changed her position.

CHERYL. I'm not scared of Mrs Ryan. She's just a mum trying to do her best for her son.

SARA. I'm not that scary. Am I, Connor?

CONNOR. Nah.

**4.8**

SARA. Hey, matey.

CONNOR. Yes, Mum.

SARA. D'you remember when you used to call me Muv-aaaar all the time?

CONNOR. Yes, Mum.

SARA. It drove me round the bend.

CONNOR. Why, Mum?

SARA. Dunno.

*Pause.*

I just wish I could hear it again.

*Pause.*

CONNOR. Mum.

SARA. Yes, matey.

CONNOR. Why did I die, Mum?

SARA. That's what we're trying to find out.

*Pause.*

CONNOR. And why did you send me to Slade House, Mum?

SARA. Because I thought it would be the best place for you.

CONNOR. But it wasn't, was it, Mum? It wasn't the best place.

*Pause.*

SARA. No, matey, it wasn't.

CONNOR. I should have stayed at home, shouldn't I, Mum?

SARA. Yes, you should have, matey.

CONNOR. But I didn't, did I, Mum?

SARA. No, matey, you didn't.

CONNOR. That's a shame, isn't it, Mum?

SARA. Yes. A terrible shame. I'm sorry, I'm so, so sorry.

*They hug.*

## PART FIVE: THE INQUEST, TAKING THE STAND

### 5.1

RICH. The inquest lasted two weeks and, somehow, we got into a routine.

SARA. Every evening we'd fall out of the courtroom into the pub across the road for a pint. Then friends would come around with food, endless chats in the kitchen. More plans. More laughter. More howling. Then knackered and into bed.

RICH. The legal team would email us submissions overnight, witness questions, the lot.

SARA. And the next morning we'd sit on the bus watching everyday life going on around us.

RICH. See that, love, a dog tied up outside Connor's old school?

SARA. People with their faces glued to Facebook. Kids going to school. The life we used to lead. Before the walls closed in.

RICH. Day four.

PAUL BOWEN QC. Morning, all. Now, look, and this is grim, but the Coroner has just been told about an earlier death at Slade House. A fifty-seven-year-old man, Henry Chilton. In 2006. With some of the same staff on duty.

RICH. What?

CHARLOTTE. And he died in the very same bath as Connor.

RICH. You're kidding?

CHARLOTTE. No, we have photographs.

SARA. The same bloody – ?

CHARLOTTE. Yes.

CONNOR. Wow, Mum, wow.

SARA. Exactly. Wow.

PAUL BOWEN QC. You see, eight long months after Connor's death, Dr Murphy suddenly remembered all about it. A report was written at the time which raised issues about the steepness of the baths and Southern Health launched an internal investigation. But, of course, they didn't act on its findings or say anything in public.

SARA. What were we meant to do with this news?

The idea that Dr Murphy suddenly remembered this is complete bollocks. Surely the fact that both of them died in the same bath was common knowledge. At least two staff members were there on both days.

RICH. But it was later decided that this didn't need to be investigated further because, quote, 'Henry Chilton's death was self-evidently from natural causes'.

SARA. The fact is that both Henry and Connor died of indifference, and their deaths were just tossed aside. Form-ticking, a phone call or two, and a quick wrapping up of loose ends with a grubby little tag saying, 'Couldn't give a shit.'

*Pause.*

And that's what so many people are up against. And it never stops.

*Pause.*

It never bloody stops.


### 5.2

ROSIE. It was finally time for Mum to take the stand.

SARA. Giving evidence was vile. There were no wigs or gowns, and I wasn't on trial, but the whole thing was – well, I told myself to keep calm, answer the questions and, for fuck's sake, not fucking swear. Which was pretty hard, I can tell you.

RICH. The jury had been fed a whole load of shite about Connor's monstrous mother:

ALAN JENKINS QC. Good morning, I'm Alan Jenkins QC and I'm acting for Dr Murphy. I'd like us to focus on three areas. First, why couldn't Connor be left alone at home?

ROSIE. In other words, Mum shouldn't have been working full time.

ALAN JENKINS QC. Second, Mrs Ryan could easily have got hold of Dr Murphy's telephone number and asked about her treatment of Connor. Why didn't she?

RICH. As if that would have solved anything.

ALAN JENKINS QC. And, third, the communications between Mrs Ryan and the professionals at Slade House. They were hardly constructive. This, for example, is from May 2013, where Charlotte Sweeney –

RICH. The occupational therapist.

ALAN JENKINS QC. – indicates that she made a telephone call to Mrs Ryan to discuss the patterns of her son's seizures. Do you remember this call?

SARA. I do.

ALAN JENKINS QC. Apparently, you told Ms Sweeney that your son had had tonic-clonic seizures and might have had absence seizures?

SARA. I wouldn't have said that.

ALAN JENKINS QC. Why not?

SARA. I would have said he *definitely* had absence seizures. On several occasions.

ALAN JENKINS QC. But was there any difficulty in sharing your knowledge? It seems to me – and the jury may agree – that there was a striking lack of rapport between you and the hard-working staff on the Unit.

RICH. Implying that because Sara was so impossible to deal with nobody realised that they should supervise Connor when he was in the bath.

ALAN JENKINS QC. After all, we've heard Cheryl, an innocent young student nurse, say that she was terrified of you. She heard you shouting at a consultant.

SARA. I asked Dr Murphy a simple question, in front of a room full of people, and it's minuted that I didn't shout.

ALAN JENKINS QC. So, she's wrong?

SARA. She is.

ALAN JENKINS QC. So now, Mrs Ryan, turning to your somewhat controversial blog. The jury will see a blog post in which you refer to a certain 'Dr Crapshite'. Would you care to explain to whom this refers?

SARA. This was in an account of my calls to the crisis line after Connor punched Big Sue in the face, when the psychiatrist said she couldn't help.

ALAN JENKINS QC. And did you imagine that this would facilitate an easy rapport with staff?

SARA. I've no idea. I do know they were anonymous. Dr Crapshite wasn't anyone in particular, it was just the whole frustrating process.

ALAN JENKINS QC. And I gather your charming nickname for the Southern Health Trust is 'Sloven'?

SARA. It is.

ALAN JENKINS QC. And do you think that that contributes to positive communications?

SARA. They killed my son, Mr Jenkins. There are stronger words I could have used.

ALAN JENKINS QC. That'll be all, thank you.

*Pause.*

RICH. Or what about this:

RODERICK JAMES QC. Good morning, Dr Ryan. My name's Roderick James QC, and I'm representing the Unit manager of Slade House. The inquest would be interested to hear why you didn't tell the Unit that Connor needed to be observed in the bath. Do you accept that you never mentioned this requirement nor the fact that you did it at home?

SARA. That's right, I didn't.

RODERICK JAMES QC. Interesting.

SARA. So, there you have it. Through a combination of working full time, writing a blog, using the words 'Dr Crapshite', calling the Trust 'Sloven' and failing to tell specialist staff to observe a young man with epilepsy in the bath, I killed my son. I wanted to climb out of the witness box and grab the smug bastard by the throat.

The fact is, Mr James, I'd no more have asked the staff to observe Connor in the bath than I'd tell a teacher not to let kids play on the motorway on a school outing.

RODERICK JAMES QC. I see.

SARA. It was lunch and I stumbled out into the streets, completely numb. I wasn't allowed to talk to anyone – not Rich, not the kids, no one – until I'd finished. And I ate a cardboard sandwich, went back in and there were no more questions.


## 5.3

RICH. The Coroner gave a detailed summing up and the jury was sent out to deliberate.

SARA. We went to the pub and got an early night.

RICH. We had no idea how long they'd take. The next morning, the flat screen in the reception announced, 'The Late Connor Sparrowhawk Inquest'. We sat there, numb. Someone told us that the jury had reached their conclusion and we went back in.

*Pause.*

The Coroner entered. We stood up and bowed our heads.

*Pause.*

The jury filed in.

*Pause.*

And we waited for the lead juror to speak.

LEAD JUROR (*reading*). 'We've established that Connor Sparrowhawk died at Slade House, a STATT Unit run by Southern Health, on 4 July 2013.

He died by drowning following an epileptic seizure while in the bath, which was contributed to by neglect.

There were very serious failings, both in terms of systems in place to ensure adequate assessment, or care and risk management of epilepsy in patients with learning disabilities.

Contributory factors include:'

VOICE 1. 'A lack of clinical leadership on the Unit.'

VOICE 2. 'A lack of adequate training and guidance for nursing staff in epilepsy.'

VOICE 3. 'A very serious failing in relation to Connor's bathing arrangement.'

LEAD JUROR. 'Other failings include:'

VOICE 1. 'The failure to complete an adequate history of Connor's epilepsy or an adequate epilepsy risk assessment at admission.'

LEAD JUROR. 'Evidence also exists of inadequate communication with Connor's family and between staff regarding Connor's epilepsy care, needs and risks.'

SARA. We'd done it. Somehow. We'd done it. A unanimous judgment.

CONNOR. You did it, Mum.

SARA. No, we did it, Connor. We all did it. All of us together,

CONNOR. Cool.

SARA. But all I really felt was emptiness. Relief yes, but disbelief that we'd been proved right. How could it be true?

I could breathe again. But only just.

*Pause.*

There was a cobbled together press conference in the car park outside and Charlotte read out a brief statement. Then, this:

JOURNALIST. Mrs Ryan, what do you feel about the apology you've received from Southern Health?

SARA. What apology?

JOURNALIST. Oh, I thought –

RICH. We've not heard an apology. Nobody's apologised to us. It shows what sort of organisation they are. They just put it out to protect their reputation. That's not a real apology.

JOURNALIST. Oh I see.

SARA. The journalist had obviously not been paying attention. Or listening to the bullshit Sloven had been feeding them.

Victoria MacDonald on Channel 4 News got it. Or as Michael Buchanan from the BBC said:

MICHAEL BUCHANAN. 'Every time Southern Health Trust had a choice, they always took the wrong path.'

SARA. And so we all went off to a tapas restaurant, drank too much sangria, and took loads of selfies. There was a piece on the BBC which showed just how much the kids loved their brother. Which reminded me what this was all about. And we staggered off to bed: tipsy, elated, tearful.

ALL *sing the first verse of 'What a Wonderful World'.*

## PART SIX: JUSTICE

### 6.1

SARA. Your grave's getting quite a collection of buses, matey. It's in the woodland bit which isn't supposed to have stuff in it, but the cemetery police look the other way.

CONNOR. Cemetery police, Mum? Are there cemetery police?

SARA. Not real police, but people in charge of the cemetery.

CONNOR. Why do they look the other way, Mum?

SARA. Oh, I dunno. I suppose the grave of an eighteen-year-old boy with a few buses and trucks, a plastic policeman and a ring of seashells isn't that big a deal.

CONNOR. Cool!

SARA. Yep. Just like you, matey: totally cool.

### 6.2

RICH. But the end of the inquest wasn't the end of the campaign. Because this was about more than just Connor. And soon the BBC published a leaked copy of the Mazar Report.

MARY ANN BRUCE. Our report presents a lot of numbers. The team recognises that each one represents a loved one and we would like to offer our condolences to the families of every person referred to.

We found an astonishing lack of leadership, focus and time spent in the reporting and investigating these deaths.

While 30% of all deaths in Adult Mental Health were investigated, less than 1% of deaths in Learning Disability Services were investigated.

SARA. Less than 1%. That's two out of three hundred and twenty seven. Connor and one other. Edward Hartley.

MARY ANN BRUCE. Timeliness is a major concern; it took on average ten months from an incident to closing an investigation. Furthermore, Southern Health Trust could not demonstrate a comprehensive, systematic approach to learning from such deaths.

## 6.3

RICH. The media got interested. At first Sara was reluctant to talk and Charlotte answered any requests.

SARA. But it was soon clear that I had to step up.

JAYNE MCCUBBIN. They want 'Mum'. I'm sure you understand.

*Projection.*

SARA. This was me on *BBC Breakfast* after a night of no sleep and blind terror. And there's Connor's beautiful face.

JAYNE MCCUBBIN. Is it upsetting?

SARA. Not really. The world needed to know.

And the world still needs to know. Ten long years later. And that's what you deserved, matey.

CONNOR. Did I, Mum?

SARA. Yes, you did.

CONNOR. And Mum.

SARA. Yes, matey,

CONNOR. Do you remember me, Mum?

SARA. Every day.

CONNOR. Every day, Mum?

SARA. Every single day. And that's what this is all about. You.

CONNOR. Me, Mum?

SARA. But now it's about more than just you.

CONNOR. More than just me, Mum?

SARA. Yes, so many other young dudes. Look.

*Projection: a roll call of names.*

All with the full range of humanity and gorgeousness. All dead. All ghosts. Beautiful, startling ghosts.

*Pause.*

I won't forget you, Connor. Never.

CONNOR. Cool, Mum.

*Pause.*

Cool.

## 6.4

ROSIE. Not everything was so positive. This was on Mum's phone. Number withheld.

VOICEMAIL MESSAGE. Hi, this is a message for Dr Sara Ryan. Um, I've been seeing on the media about your son, your poor son who died in the care of Southern Health. I work for Southern Health, and I feel awful that you lost him. I'm so sorry, it's tragic, and I hope you find some closure after the report, the CQC report today, but I do think you're being vindictive. You're a vindictive cow. On TV all the time slagging off the NHS. You know, as much as anyone, that Southern Health only took over those Units recently, in the months before your son died. And you know with your intelligent background, that it takes a while to make changes, and I think it's become a witch hunt and you want attention. But you're vindictive and unpleasant, and a nasty cow.

SARA. Nice, eh?

RICH. I'm going to call the police.

GEORGE JULIAN. And let's put it on the blog.

**6.5**

RICH. Sloven then called an extraordinary Board Meeting to, quote, 'discuss the Mazar Report'.

SARA. It was attended by Katrina Percy, their 'hard-working Chief Executive', who's 'happy to answer any questions'.

KATRINA PERCY (*sunnily*). Morning, everyone.

SARA. We all turned up. The whole campaign. But it was a typical shambles. The Sloven suits sat at a u-shaped table at one end of the room. We all stood or sat on the floor at the other. I don't think they realised how many of us would show up.

GEORGE JULIAN. After three hours talking among themselves the chairman finally addressed us:

SOUTHERN HEALTH CHAIR. I'd like to open this very interesting discussion to questions from the floor.

TOM *puts up his hand.*

Yes, young man.

TOM. Oh, hello, I'm Connor's younger brother, and I just wanted to say that I thought it was totally inappropriate of you to say you *might* have added to our grief as a family, when you so totally piled it on.

SOUTHERN HEALTH CHAIR. I see.

*Pause.*

Katrina?

KATRINA PERCY. Well –

*Pause.*

I'm, erm –

*Pause.*

I'm sorry. That's all.

TOM. And you know that's the first time I've heard an apology, and I'm only sixteen and this is a room full of grown-ups.

And it's not easy, you know. But I had to do it because you guys never apologised. Not once.

*Pause.*

SOUTHERN HEALTH CHAIR.Yes, the lady over there.

BECCA. Morning, I'm Becca, a friend of Connor's mum, and what I want to know is have we come to the right place? I mean, you lot don't seem to know anything about anything.

SARA. They couldn't answer that. And then Sarah Snow, who was so nervous she'd written it down, asked a question:

SARAH SNOW (*reads*.) As a parent of a young person with autism and learning disabilities, the Mazar Report feels like a nightmare. We've been treated with institutional and personal contempt. You've created a situation where the services the people need are no longer accessible because individuals and families don't have confidence in their safety.

SARA. And finally, Shaun Picken stood up. He has learning disabilities.

SHAUN PICKEN. Look, Katrina, you were struggling. We all knew that. There are so many people around who could have helped.

*Pause.*

Why didn't you ask for help?

*Pause.*

Eh?

*Pause.*

Why didn't you?

SARA. And answer came there none.

RICH. Tom was going to be featured on TV news that evening.

SARA. I've just been told that they're going to run it at ten. Look.

*Footage.*

TOM. Was I alright?

SARA. You were fantastic.

CONNOR. Great, Tom. Wasn't he, Mum?

SARA. Absolutely.

CONNOR, TOM, OWEN, WILL *and* ROSIE *sing the chorus of 'All the Young Dudes' by David Bowie.*

TOM. It could have been our theme tune.

## PART SEVEN: CRIME AND PUNISHMENT

### 7.1

DC CHARLIE ELLIS. Mrs Ryan?

SARA. Yes.

DC CHARLIE ELLIS. Charlie Ellis, Detective Constable, Thames Valley Police.

RICH. This was in the relatives' room at the hospital, the morning Connor died.

DC CHARLIE ELLIS. I just wanted to say that although we've not yet been able to investigate properly what happened it doesn't look like there are any suspicious circumstances. Just a terrible accident, I'm afraid. I'm so –

SARA. It's not an accident.

DC CHARLIE ELLIS. We've talked to the staff –

SARA. You see, Charlie had already been exposed to the myth of 'natural causes'.

RICH. But, like all of us, he learnt to ask questions. And, by March 2014, we thought there should be a corporate manslaughter charge and the police gathered evidence to see if the bar for prosecution had been reached.

SARA. The three of us went to see Charlie in his office. Police kit everywhere. Connor would have loved it.

DC CHARLIE ELLIS. I just wanted to give an update on your anonymous phone message. I've managed to track the woman down. She's a member of staff at Southern Health and, well, she's got challenges of her own. The whole place is under so much pressure –

RICH. I'm sorry, but why should we bend over backwards after all the shite they've put us through?

DC CHARLIE ELLIS. Well, yes.

TOM. Charlie – sorry, PC Charlie – can I ask a question?

DC CHARLIE ELLIS. Of course, Tom.

TOM. If my mum had done to my brother what the guys at
Sloven did she'd be arrested, wouldn't she?

DC CHARLIE ELLIS. Almost certainly.

TOM. But not this lot?

DC CHARLIE ELLIS. No.

TOM. Why not?

DC CHARLIE ELLIS. A good question, Tom. A very good
question

SARA. And then, in February 2017, Charlie came round with
some bad news.

DC CHARLIE ELLIS. I'm afraid the CPS has advised that the
evidence doesn't meet the 'gross negligence' bar and that the
case is closed. 'Negligence', yes, but not 'gross negligence'.
I'm really sorry.

RICH. S'alright. You did what you can.

SARA. At least Charlie talked to us as human beings.

GEORGE JULIAN. Luckily, health and safety law is different
from criminal law –

DC CHARLIE ELLIS. And offers a better chance of conviction.

GEORGE JULIAN. And so, in May 2017, we persuaded
Norman Lamb to put pressure on the Health and Safety
Executive to prosecute.

NORMAN LAMB. 'Better late than never.'

GEORGE JULIAN. As he put it.

## 7.2

RICH. By 2016, Southern Health had lost the contract to provide learning disability services in Oxfordshire and Slade House stood empty. Then they put it up for sale.

SARA. So, a bunch of us went to see Jeremy Hunt to talk about it and raise the bigger question of the neglect and poor care of learning-disabled people. He was late.

JEREMY HUNT. Oh, hello, do come in, I'm delighted to meet you. So sorry to hear about what happened. How ghastly. Do sit here, it's the most comfortable chair in my office, er, can Mary get you some tea?

SARA. We'd been promised an hour – it ended being half that, and most was 'grieving mother' bullshit – and, surprise, surprise, it was soon clear he wasn't going to listen.

## 7.3

CONNOR. Mum, d'you remember how much I loved mermaids?

SARA. I do.

CONNOR. And, Mum, d'you remember when Big Sue took me to throw a message in a bottle in the river?

SARA. I do.

CONNOR. 'Dear Mermaids, do you exist or don't you? From Connor.'

SARA. That's right, matey.

CONNOR. And I got a letter back, didn't I, Mum? And a pouch with some shells in it? Remember?

SARA. I do, matey, I do.

CONNOR. 'Dear Connor, we do exist, and we want you to sleep with the shells under your pillow to help you dream about us.'

SARA. That's right.

CONNOR. And I got postcards, didn't I, Mum? From all sorts of places. Greece, Italy, France.

SARA. You did, matey. Which – amazingly – coincided with the teachers' holidays.

CONNOR. And remember, Mum, I really liked *The Inbetweeners*, didn't I, and I went to TRAX, and I did mechanic training? Remember? Cool overalls. But I didn't like all the smoking, did I, Mum?

SARA. No, you didn't, matey.

CONNOR. But I started pretending to smoke, didn't I, Mum? Like this.

SARA. You did.

CONNOR. And, Mum, is it true, after I died, they gave you a prize?

SARA. They did, matey.

CONNOR. And the actor, Mum, what's he called, from *The Inbetweeeners*, did he – ?

SARA. Simon Bird.

CONNOR. Yeah. Did he give it to you, Mum?

SARA. He did, but Richy Rich and the gang picked it up because I was away. But I wouldn't have been surprised if a mermaid had turned up too. You see, there are good people in the world. There have to be.


**7.4**

RICH. Meanwhile, back in the much less wonderful real world, there were changes at Southern Health. A new chairman, Tim Smart, had been appointed. Seemed a smart appointment.

TIM SMART. Delighted. I know what you've been through.

SARA. But my head hit the floor when he said he'd not read the Mazar Report.

TIM SMART. I'm afraid not.

SARA. Oh, why not?

TIM SMART. Because it's wrong.

SARA. Wrong?

TIM SMART. Completely.

SARA. How can you know it's wrong if you haven't read it?

RICH. And a few weeks later –

TIM SMART. 'After a thorough investigation.'

RICH. – he announced that –

TIM SMART. – while the Trust could have acted in a more united way, there is no evidence of negligence or incompetence on the part of any individual board member.

RICH. But then we heard that a training outfit called Talent Works had pocketed five million quid from Sloven to deliver a contract originally worth three hundred thousand. What's more, its boss was an old mate of Katrina Percy's.

SARA. And soon the *Daily Mail* went after Percy herself.

TIM SMART. The Board can announce that Ms Percy will be stepping down as Chief Executive but will move to a new role at Southern Health for which she is uniquely qualified.

SARA. ?

TIM SMART. At the same salary.

SARA. £240,000 a year. Plus pension. Was it publicly advertised?

TIM SMART. An internal appointment.

SARA. So, no due process?

See that? A public organisation sticking two fingers up to the rest of us.

RICH. Tim Smart resigned in September 2016, citing –

TIM SMART. 'Personal reasons.'

RICH. – but of course it was his support for Percy.

SARA. And, in October, I was in Berlin and got a call.

MAIL ON SUNDAY. Ms Ryan, Mail on Sunday. I thought you'd like to know that Katrina Percy has resigned on a full year's salary and won't be allowed to work in the NHS for a further year. Do you have any comment?

SARA. What could I say?


## 7.5

SARA. Blimey, you were such a cute baby. So blooming cute. Those cheeks. And a smile to light up the world. And that laugh. That bloody laugh.

CONNOR. Mum?

SARA. Yes?

CONNOR. Was I born in a bath, Mum?

SARA. You were, matey. In a bath. At home.

CONNOR. And, Mum?

SARA. Yes

CONNOR. Did I die in a bath, Mum?

*Pause.*

Mum?

*Pause.*

Mum?

SARA. Yes, you did. You died in a bath.

CONNOR. Why, Mum?

SARA. I don't know. And I still don't know. I just don't know.

## EPILOGUE: THE FUNERAL

### Epilogue 1

SARA. Finally, two weeks after he died, the dreaded day arrived.

TOM. We've got some film of it. Not great quality. But it's real.

*Film of people on an old Routemaster going to the cemetery.*

SARA. And before we set out, I took a picture of the four kids in the kitchen. Look.

*Projection.*

Dressed in bright colours. About to walk behind their brother's coffin to his grave.

RICH. It's not right, is it?

*Pause.*

ROSIE. We walked together. Arm in arm.

WILL. I'll never forget it.

OWEN. Feels like yesterday.

TOM. Holding tight.

SARA. And it was so hot. Again.

*Pause.*

Remember Big Sue? Well, she helped carry the coffin to the grave. She understood.

*Looking at the film.*

There she is, see?

*Pause.*

And then we left him.

*Pause.*

We left him in the ground.

Goodbye, Connor. Goodbye.

We love you so much.

*Very long pause. Nothing happens. Finally:*

And so we walked back to the bus. The six of us. Together.


## Epilogue 2

WILL. 'Connor's do' was amazing.

ROSIE. Yeah, well, Becca and Fran found this ballroom type place at the Cowley Works. Cheap bar. Great music. Really cool.

SARA. The perfect venue for something that should never have happened.

OWEN. It was fun, believe it or not.

RICH. We're so proud of these kids.

SARA. You wouldn't believe how proud.

TOM. I was thirteen when Connor died. He was my big brother. And I loved him.

ROSIE. And he was my little brother. And I'll always love him. The thing is Connor made me feel safe. I don't know why, but he did. Comfortable. And safe.

SARA. We all loved him. That's the truth.

ROSIE. And we always will.


## Epilogue 3

SARA. In 2018 Southern Health was fined a record two million quid for breaching health and safety laws. We drank to that, I can tell you.

But not much else, I'm afraid. Because people like Connor are still left to live, and sometimes die, in squalor: neglected, ignored and worse.

And so, the fight goes on. It has to.

*Pause.*

Connor died ten long years ago now. The kids have grown up and we don't live in Oxford any more. Everything's changed. But if I close my eyes I can still hear his laughter ringing in my ears. And that's what this is all about. Laughter and love.

And laughter and love can –

Look.

*Projection of Connor laughing and then the Justice Quilt.*

ALL *sing the first two verses of 'What a Wonderful World'.*

*End.*

**A Nick Hern Book**

*Laughing Boy* first published in Great Britain as a paperback original in 2024 by Nick Hern Books Limited, The Glasshouse, 49a Goldhawk Road, London W12 8QP, in association with Jermyn Street Theatre, London

*Laughing Boy* copyright © 2024 Stephen Unwin

*Justice for Laughing Boy* (original book) copyright © 2017 Sara Ryan, published by Jessica Kingsley Publishers Ltd, with this adaptation published with permission through PLSclear

Stephen Unwin has asserted his right to be identified as the author of this adaptation

Cover image by Ciaran Walsh (CIWA Design)

Designed and typeset by Nick Hern Books, London
Printed in Great Britain by Mimeo Ltd, Huntingdon, Cambridgeshire PE29 6XX

A CIP catalogue record for this book is available from the British Library

ISBN 978 1 83904 353 6

www.nickhernbooks.co.uk/environmental-policy

**www.nickhernbooks.co.uk**

facebook.com/nickhernbooks

twitter.com/nickhernbooks